The Spooky S

By Phillip M. Drake

Introduction

I have always had an interest in the paranormal ever since I was a child, and I have read many books on the subject. There have been a number of books about hauntings in the Hampshire and Isle of Wight area in recent years, however, I felt that it was time for an update.

In this book, you will find a collection of hauntings ranging from the historical and well-known to the new and more modern. This is by no means a definitive collection, although I have attempted to include as many famous haunted locations as possible, whilst adding just enough new stories to add some much needed freshness.

I have been disappointed with the layouts of some of the other books on the subject, as well as the lack of an eBook option. Therefore, I have listed the haunted location in an easy to navigate A to Z format, with separate sections for Hampshire and the Isle of Wight.

Just one final note...

If, after working through this book, you are spurred on to go and visit some of the haunted locations listed here, please bear in mind that some locations are private dwellings, and the owners may not be too impressed with you arriving at their home unannounced. On the flip-side, there are still plenty of locations that are open to the public, especially the stately homes and public houses, so you should still find plenty of places for a ghost hunt.

I hope you enjoy reading this book as much as I enjoyed researching and writing it.

Phillip Drake, 2015

Contents

Hampshire

Isle of Wight

HAMPSHIRE

Being the largest county in the South of England means that Hampshire has more than its fair share of haunted locations, and with large population centres such as Basingstoke to the north and Southampton and Portsmouth to the south, many people have experienced ghostly goings-on through the centuries.

The historic city of Winchester, the ancient capital of England, is just one of many haunted locations throughout the county, and with such a rich history, Hampshire can certainly lay claim to being one of the most haunted counties in Britain.

From phantom nurses, soldiers, sailors, and even the odd ghostly dog, there is something for even the most hardened sceptic to think about.

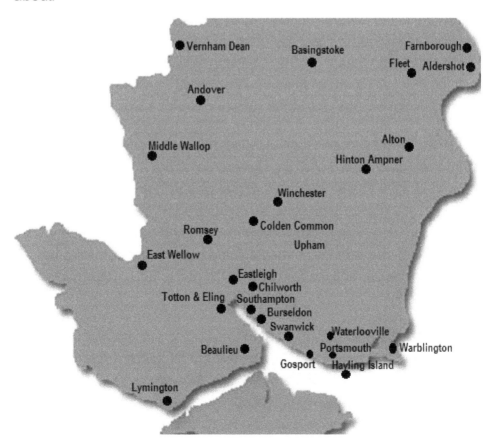

Aldershot

The Grey Lady of the Cambridge Military Hospital

Opened in July 1879 and named after Prince George the Duke of Cambridge, the Cambridge Military Hospital was at the forefront of modern plastic surgery techniques, especially during the First World War.

As the need to cater for ill and injured soldiers declined in the immediate years after the Second World War, the rules were changed to allow the treatment of civilians. However, by 1996, the costs associated with running the hospital were becoming prohibitive, and after asbestos was discovered in the walls the decision was made to close the hospital for good.

It is said that the hospital is haunted by a ghost of a grey lady, who would often be seen on the upper floors of the building usually between wards 10 and 14. Such was the reputation of this part of the building that care assistants and nurses would often avoid this part of the corridor by walking the stairs between wards 1 and 7.

The exact identity of the Grey Lady is not known, however, legend has it that she was a member of the Queen Alexandra's Royal Army Nursing Corps. The story goes that she was a Sister who accidentally gave one of the soldier patients an overdose and he later died as a result of the error. The nurse was so traumatised and guilt ridden by her error that she later committed suicide by throwing herself to her death from the upper floor walkway, which at the time of the incident was open plan.

Sightings of the grey lady were said to coincide with patients who were gravely ill or near to death, and it is said that she appeared in order to give patients comfort in their final few moments. People who have seen her have stated that the corridor would always be cold, even on the hottest days or when the heating was turned up high, and there was always an accompanying smell of lavender in the air.

With the hospital long since closed and the buildings falling into disrepair, one wonders if the grey lady still forlornly walks the corridors in search of patients who are no longer there. Since the closure of the CMH there have not been any new reported sightings of the grey lady, however, some Ministry of Defence Police officers who now patrol the disused site often comment that the hairs on the back of their necks stand on end for no apparent reason when they are near the site.

The Alma Lane Ghost

It is said that on a windy night in the Alma Lane area of Aldershot you can hear the thumping of boots and the clanking of a musket. These mysterious noises have been attributed to the death of a military messenger, who was said to have been killed by a couple of brigands whilst delivering a message regarding the victory at the battle of Waterloo.

Cambridge Hospital, Aldershot

Alton

The Ghost of Fanny Adams

Alton is the home of a number of ghosts with one of the most famous being the spirit of poor Fanny Adams, who was kidnapped and murdered by Frederick Baker in 1869. The murder was big news at the time, and the name of Fanny Adams has passed into the English language to mean something of little value or worth. This was due to the fact that British seaman were first given mutton to eat in 1869, not long after the dismembered remains of Fanny Adams were discovered, and "Fanny Adams" became slang for mutton or stew. Not long afterwards use of the phrase changed to mean nothing at all and was later shortened to "Sweet F.A."

The remains of Fanny Adams were found scattered around the hills above Alton and it is said that her ghost has been seen playing in the area where she was killed.

The Crown Hotel

One other haunted site of note in Alton is the Crown Hotel, which is the location of an unusual canine haunting. A number of visitors to the hotel have noticed that a specific chimney breast in the building would cause dogs to bark and back away, whilst all the time staring at the chimney breast as if something was there. Chillingly, a former landlord and several regular patrons described how they would often hear what sounded like an animal scratching from within the fireplace.

There are many different stories regarding the spooky scratching noises that emanate from behind the fireplace, and these include the story of a drunken man who killed his whining dog by picking it up by its hind legs and dashing its head against the chimney breast. Of course, no one really knows the origins of these sounds, but one story suggests that in 1967, workmen who were renovating that area of the bar uncovered the remains of a dog hidden in the original dining room hearth.

The Crown Hotel, Alton

Andover

The Andover Poltergeist

When Paranormal Investigators Tony Cornell and Alan Gauld documented 500 poltergeist-type cases back in the late 1970s they found that most involved rapping noises, often described as knocks and thumps for which no source could be found.

The paranormal activity had started without warning, the two Andrews girls in bed one night heard a curious tapping noise coming from somewhere in the room. This happened on several consecutive nights. The raps seemed to coming from within the wall, at first the girls thought the noise was coming from the house next door. Soon they began to realize that the noise was responding to them, even when they whispered questions so quietly that no one outside the room could possibly hear.

The girls started to communicate with it, by asking questions and getting it to knock once for yes, two for no, and three for don't know. For more complex queries it would rap out the letter of the alphabet (five knocks for E, 13 for M, etc).

Mr Colvin made a total of nine visits to the property over a ten week period. As well as interviewing the family about the origins of the case he had plenty of opportunity to hear the raps himself and establish that they were not the result of trickery or other visible cause. The focus of the activity seemed to have been Theresa, the younger of the two girls aged 12. Colvin also established to his own satisfaction that the source had intelligence of a sort, calling itself Eric Waters, although it did not seem to have provided any coherent information beyond that.

A medium that Mr Andrews had previously invited to the property had claimed the noises were being made by a young boy whose body was buried under the floorboards. Further investigation by the family failed to turn up anyone of that name who had lived in the area.

Colvin attempted a small experiment, persuading 'Eric' to transfer the noises from the wall of the room to the headboard of Theresa's bed. Mrs Andrews asked Eric, to knock on the headboard. This was followed by a very soft tap which was heard by all Mrs Andrews her Husband and Mr Colvin. Mrs Andrews repeated the request and the raps were progressively louder on the headboard.

The Andrews family seem to have been rather ambivalent about the case, enjoying the novelty of communicating with an unseen entity, but becoming frightened when the knocks and raps turned into loud banging's, especially when they went on for hours and deprived them of sleep. By Colvin's last visit the phenomena seemed to have faded out. While the family treated Eric as a deceased spirit, Colvin's view was that the case fitted the pattern of repressed emotion in the living, although there was no outward sign of this, the family being apparently happy and stable.

A medium that Mr Andrews had invited to the property had claimed the noises were being made by a young boy whose body was buried under the floorboards. Further investigation by the family failed to turn up anyone of that name who had lived in the area.

The Phantom Coach and Horses of the A303

The road that is now the A303 can trace its history back for centuries, as it was originally a stagecoach route between London and the Southwest, and it seems that these stagecoaches are still using this particular route.

Prior to the bypass being built there were two reports of vehicles being involved in near misses with a spectral coach. The first happened near to Longparish where a startled motorist drove his car off the road when his car headlights illuminated a coach and four horses that were heading straight towards him. The second incident took place one dark night in the 1960's near to Wherwell when a motorist, who was heading home from Southampton, had to break sharply in order to avoid a coach and horses that appeared in front of him. The startled motorist said that the apparition disappeared as quickly as it had arrived, leaving the poor man in a state of shock.

During the construction of the bypass, workmen often heard the clip-clop of horse's hooves that would get louder and louder as though they were getting nearer until they stopped suddenly, yet despite looking around, there was no sign of any horses in the surrounding area.

The White Hart Hotel

The White Hart Hotel is more 300 years old, and is said to be inhabited by a number of spirits and not all of them of the alcoholic variety. The first is the apparition of an attractive woman who is dressed in either a dark green cloak or dress. It seems as though she favours room 20 and it is here that she manifested herself to the same female residence in the space of one evening in the 1960's. The poor woman was so unsettled by the experience that she checked out the following morning. The green lady as she is known has also been seen gliding along the corridors of the hotel, although no one knows whether she is responsible for the ghostly footsteps often heard in other areas of the hotel.

It seems as though the green lady is not alone, as there have also been other reports of phantoms in the hotel. These other haunting have been attributed to another man and a woman who seem to be more interested in haunting the ground floor of the hotel rather than the upper floors. It was a barman working alone one day who witnessed the phantom pair, describing them as being almost translucent and an off-white colour, and they disappeared before his eyes, leaving him more than a little perturbed. It is not known which of the three spooks once terrorised a poor young maid who described how she was chased up the stairs and along a corridor by some disembodied footsteps. After rushing into her own room and locking the door, the footsteps stopped outside her door, and it was quite some time before the owners could entice the girl to leave her room.

Red Rice House

Red Rice is a small hamlet to the south-west of Andover, and the house is a Grade II listed building that dates back to 1740 or thereabouts. This house is home to another sighting of a 'Grey Lady', and grey ladies certainly seem to be a common theme in a lot of hauntings. This haunting relates to two school employees who had accommodation on one of the upper floors, who both reported severe feelings of terror in one specific area of their room.

The White Hart Hotel, Andover

Photo: Chris Talbot

Basingstoke

Bramshill House Police Training College

One of the most important Jacobean mansions anywhere in the UK, Bramshill House is reputed to be the home of a staggering number of ghosts, 14 in all, which is some total for one building. Currently the home to a Police training college, Bramshill House was built in the 17th century by Edward La Zouche, and it has been a Grade I listed building since 1952.

One of the many ghosts said to roam the maze of corridors and rooms in Bramshill House include a grey lady, a woman whose husband was beheaded in the 17th century for being a religious dissenter. However, the most famous ghost story associated with Bramshill House is the legend of Mistletoe Bough, which is a ghost story that has been attributed to several mansions across England.

The legend concerns a bride who whilst participating in a game of hide and seek on her wedding night, hid in an old wooden chest (although the Bramshill House version is supposed to have taken place at Christmas time) where she became trapped. Despite frantic searches no one could find her, and she was not discovered until 50 years later, still wearing her wedding dress and clutching a sprig of mistletoe. The chest that she is said to have died in, used to be on display in the entrance hall of Bramshill House, and may still be there.

Many people have experienced strange phenomena when visiting the house. A Mr. Clarke, who was working in the house, explained that he witnessed an attractive woman who was walking in a forlorn fashion through the library. He explained that she appeared to be around 18 years of age, and that she appeared to be dressed in an old fashioned long gown that swept the ground as she walked.

Other people have experienced unexplainable phenomena such as sudden drops in temperature, an aroma of Lily of the Valley perfume, and fleeting glimpses of a greyish-white lady on the stairs near to the chapel.

Other ghosts that are said to frequent this magnificent building include a little man dressed in green, who is only visible to children, and it is thought that he is Henry Cope, who was the eccentric gardener and a close friend of George III. Apparently, Henry Cope had a thing for the colour green, and he would only wear green coloured clothes, eat green coloured foods, and all of his rooms, carriages and even the horses were adorned with green.

In addition to the green man, other ghosts include the spirit of a deer keeper who was shot accidently by an archbishop, a nun, and a woman in Stuart period clothing who has been seen in the chapel area.

The Interior of Bramshill House

Cliddesden Station

Not far from Basingstoke lies the hamlet of Cliddesden, which was once home to a small station halt on the Basingstoke to Alton Light Railway in the early part of the 20th Century. The line eventually closed to all traffic in 1932, but it did survive long enough to become the home of the fictional station of Buggleskelly in the 1937 Will Hay film Oh, Mr. Porter. The film itself is loosely based on the Arnold Ridley play The Ghost Train, and now it seems as though fiction and the paranormal have joined forces, as many local people have stated that they often hear the sound of a steam train passing by along the route of the old line.

The Haymarket Theatre

One of three main theatres in Basingstoke, The Haymarket is said to be haunted by a number of ghosts of former performers, as well as many others. The building that now houses the theatre was originally a corn exchange, and it also found use as an ambulance station, a bowling alley, a discotheque and even as an ice rink, before finally being converted to a theatre. Workers and visitors have reported seeing a number of apparitions, which include a man in a tricorn hat, a lady in grey, a little girl, and a whistling ghost which is heard but never seen. On one occasion, a team of ghost hunters encountered a sudden drop in temperature in the auditorium, before several members witnessed a woman in a white Victorian dress who was walking serenely across the stage. They also encountered the sudden smell of burning wood in an area of the theatre that had been severely damaged by fire in the past.

The White Hart Inn

This interesting inn is home to a number of ghosts, who were apparently disturbed during renovation work in the 1960's. The disturbances include the sound of beer barrels being rolled along gravel, which on one occasion caused one of the pubs owners to investigate the possibility that thieves were making off with a barrel of beer. Footsteps have also been heard walking around the pub late at night. In the seventies, one proprietor's mother witnessed a female apparition standing in her room, whilst on another occasion, a live-in staff member witnessed a blond girl combing her hair in her bedroom mirror, before disappearing into thin air.

The Chequers Pub, Eversley

This quaint pub is situated in the village of Eversley, which is around 11 miles to the northeast of Basingstoke, and it said to be haunted by at least eight ghosts.

There have been a number of different unexplained paranormal occurrences that have been witnessed down the years, and these include; lights switching themselves on and off, unexplained cold spots, and items in the kitchen being moved by an unseen force. A previous landlord and regulars have also mentioned in the past that there was a presence of a little boy named 'Jack'.

One particularly unsettling experience happened one day in the restaurants toilets. The then landlady told local reporters that a young girl, who was visiting the pub with her parents, became separated from them, and her parents were only alerted to her disappearance when they heard her screams coming from inside the woman's washroom. Upon entering, they discovered their daughter in an extremely distressed state, and she proceeded to tell them that she had heard the voice of a woman talking to her but there was no one else in there with her.

Beaulieu

Beaulieu Abbey and Palace House

Founded in 1204 by Cistercian monks, Beaulieu Abbey and Palace House are owned by the Montagu family. It is also home to a number of unusual and unexplained events and apparitions, and can rival Bramshill House as the most haunted place in Hampshire, with ghost sightings stretching back over 100 years.

Ghostly monks have been spotted in the grounds as far back as 1886, and the sounds of Gregorian chanting are said to be audible on warm summer nights. Theses chants are said to be heard after the death of a villager, and on one occasion a fairly new resident had enquired about a service for a recently deceased fellow resident, only to be told that they must have heard the ghostly monks. Within the abbey itself, people often hear footsteps climbing the stairs and the clink of keys can be heard by monastic doorways but no one is ever seen.

Another strange happening that is connected to the death of a resident of the village is the sudden and unexplained smell of incense in the Palace House, which is often detectable in the upper rooms. Legend has it that this strong smell of incense signifies the death of a villager or that someone in the Montagu family is in peril.

The grey lady is another ghost associated with Palace House, and it is said to be the wandering spirit of Isabella, the Countess of Beaulieu who passed away in 1786. She has been spotted on numerous occasions walking along corridors and through walls of what are now the private apartments of the house. She has also been seen in the main house where startled visitors have often enquired as to why the costumed guide had not spoken to them!

Bramshott

The village of Bramshott is situated on the eastern side of the county and can trace its history back to the 13th century, and it is even named in the Doomsday Book. Thanks to its ancient history, Bramshott is apparently haunted by as many as 17 ghosts, which makes it one of the most haunted villages in Britain.

Among the ghostly inhabitants of Bramshott is the famous actor Boris Karloff who spent his final days living in a cottage in the village. Legend has it that his ghost still haunts his old home, and there have been several sightings in the lanes nearby also, although it has not been noted whether his spirit was wearing his famous Frankenstein's Monster makeup.

Several ghosts are also said to call the quaint country lanes of Bramshott home, with several sightings of various apparitions having been spotted including a cavalier, a highwayman and several people dressed in Tudor garb.

It is not just the lanes and byways of Bramshott that are home to a variety of ghosts, as there are a number of buildings that are also said to be haunted. The first is Bramshott Church, where the ghost of a little girl wearing a bonnet has been seen walking away from the church, before vanishing through the churchyard wall.

Meanwhile, the old manor house in Bramshott is home to an apparition of a number of ghosts including a Quaker, a phantom priest and a former female owner of the house.

Bursledon

Bursledon Brickworks

Built in 1897, Bursledon Brickworks is a preserved site and home to the last remaining steam powered brickworks in Britain, and visiting the site you get a real feel for the spirit of the Industrial revolution and the Victorian era. But, there are other spirits here too, and the site is said to be haunted by the ghost of a worker who was killed after seeking warmth and shelter in one of the kilns. The unfortunate man was killed when he became locked in and the kiln was lit the following morning by his unsuspecting co-workers. The strange occurrences witnessed here include the sound of disembodied whistling, voices, and footsteps. A recent séance held here resulted in a glass being moved by an unseen force, and people have also felt the presence of a large or tall figure towering over them.

Bursledon Brickworks

Photo: Chris Allen

Chilworth

<u>The Ghost of Walnut Cottage</u>

This quaint 17th century chocolate-box cottage that is situated just outside of Southampton has been reportedly haunted since the 1800's. Originally two separate cottages when it was built during the reign of King Charles II, it was eventually enlarged into one single dwelling, and it has been used as a school and a guest house during its long history.

At one stage during the 1850's the hauntings were said to be so disturbing that nobody wanted to buy the cottage, and it remained empty for a number of years. During its time as a guest house, people who stayed there were often so disturbed by what they had experienced that they left to find other accommodation in the village. So, what types of hauntings were so unnerving that people shunned this delightful old English cottage?

The first detailed reports come from the 1920's and relate to a couple from Glasgow who was staying at the cottage, which even then was still being used as a guest house. On one occasion during their stay they were both awakened in the night only to discover that the eiderdown on their bed appeared to be glowing, however, there was no heat emanating from it.

A similar incident occurred in 1939 to Mrs MacRae, the owner of the cottage, and other ghostly phenomena was also witnessed by both Mrs MacRae and her husband. One night that same year, Mr MacRae was alone in the cottage late one night and unable to sleep when he suddenly heard the sound of two men having a conversation. Looking towards a table he was shocked to discover two old men in cloth caps sitting at the table talking.

Phantom footsteps are continually being heard also, and the MacRae's had plenty of unnerving experiences with this type of phenomenon. One night in particular, Mrs MacRae was sleeping alone in the cottage when she was awoken by the sound of two people approaching the front door of the cottage. She could distinctly hear their footsteps on the path, as well as the sound of their voices. Assuming that they were travellers who were lost and in need of assistance, she got out of bed and went downstairs in order to greet them at the front door. However, when she opened the door there was no sign of anyone, and there had been no sound of anyone walking away from the cottage. Horses have also been heard approaching the cottage, but on investigation there has been no sign of any horses in the vicinity.

On other occasions, the MacRae's would often hear someone knock on the door, but when they answered it there was no one there. Also, they often heard the sound of the heavy letterbox being opened, as though something was being pushed through, but again, nothing was ever there, and the spring on the letterbox was so heavy that it was impossible for it to be moved by the wind.

The ghostly sounds do not end there, with both Mr and Mrs MacRae and visitors to their home experiencing strange and unexplained noises, both at night and during the day. Sounds of crockery smashing onto the ground went unexplained, as did the sound of footsteps and someone breathing heavy climbing the stairs. People have also heard the sound of someone washing their hands in a wash basin in a room where there were no such washing facilities.

Colden Common

The White Lady of Marwell Hall

Marwell Hall is a Grade I listed building and is part of the sprawling acres of Marwell Wildlife (formerly Marwell Zoological Park). The hall was originally built in 1320, and then rebuilt in 1816, and it is said to be haunted by a mysterious lady in white.

It has been said that the lady in white is the spirit of both Jane Seymour and Anne Boleyn. No one knows for sure, but legend has it that the ghost of the lady in white who has been seen walking along Yew Tree Walk in the grounds is that of Jane Seymour who just happened to be planning her wedding to Henry VIII whilst Anne Boleyn was being executed. Other people suggest that it is actually the ghost of the disgruntled Anne Boleyn who is searching for the two lovers in order to gain some kind of revenge. It has even be suggested that Henry actually married Jane Seymour here as the execution of Anne Boleyn was taking place at the Tower of London, before their official wedding ceremony took place back in the capital. Either way, plenty of people have stated that they have seen the lady in white, or have felt uneasy walking in that particular area.

Marwell Hall is also the second Hampshire location to be associated with the legend of the Misteltoe Bough (see Bramshill House, above), which tells of the story of the brand new bride and her wooden chest hideaway. There have been many variations and locations for this legend, ranging from Cornwall to East Anglia, and there are links to 5 locations in Hampshire alone including both Marwell Hall and Bramshill House. It seems to me, from a Hampshire point of view that Bramshill House seems to be the most likely location and that is why you will find the details about this particular legend in that section.

Crondall

All Saints Church

The ghosts of Cromwellian soldiers in full military regalia and on horseback have been witnessed for centuries in and around the grounds of All Saints Church in the small village of Crondall. The village, like many of its kind in Hampshire, is an ancient settlement that can trace its history back hundreds of years, and is mentioned in the Doomsday Book. During the English Civil War, Crondall found itself in the middle of some of the most vicious and bloodthirsty fighting to take place in Hampshire, thanks to its location close to the strategically important town of Alton. One of Cromwell's commanders, Sir William Waller, stationed a significant force of men in preparation for an attack on nearby Basing House, which was a Royalist stronghold, and they made use of All Saints Church. The Royalists often attacked the Parliamentarians in the village on a regular basis, and some of the battles were quite ferocious. Now it seems that some of the unfortunate Roundheads, who did not survive the battles, now haunt the church and its surrounds, as many men in Parliamentary uniform have been witnessed down through the years.

East Wellow

St. Margaret's Church

The ghost of Florence Nightingale has been seen either sitting on a pew or walking around the grounds of St. Margaret's Church in East Wellow where she is buried. She is accompanied in her haunting activities by Colonel William Morton, a man who was one of the signatories of the death warrant of King Charles I. Now his spirit roams the roads of East Wellow, and he has been seen walking towards St. Margaret's Church, maybe for a chat with the Lady with the Lamp.

East Wellow's final haunting comes in the form of a ghostly coach and four, which is seen trotting down some of the lanes, although not seen for a number of years, local's say that it is only ever been seen late at night.

Farnborough

The Kingsmead Shopping Centre

The town of Farnborough used to have three distinct shopping areas, Kingsmead, Queensmead and Princes mead, although Kingsmead and Queensmead have since been renovated and incorporated into one area now known as simply 'The Meads'. The Kingsmead Shopping Centre was constructed towards the tail end of the 1970's, and it is believed to have been built on the site of a house called Firgrove Cottage. Whether the demolition of the cottage and the construction of the shopping centre has stirred up some supernatural activity no one knows, but many people who have worked in some of the stores in the area have experienced unexplained phenomena.

Shopping centre employees have reported hearing disembodied footsteps and the sound of doors banging in the centre, and many people have described the distinctive sound of children running around and laughing, even when the centre has been closed.

A man who owned and ran the newsagents in the centre once described how he opened the shop early one morning, only to discover that all of the newspapers had been scattered all over the floor, covering it like a blanket of snow. There were no signs of a break-in and the man was the only person with access to the keys.

However, the most intriguing and unsettling experiences have taken place in what was once the Southern Electric Showroom. A former employee (who does not want to be identified) relates his rather unsettling experiences whilst working in the shop.

> I was working in the store in the early 1990's, although I'm not sure of the exact year as what I am about to tell you happened over a period of time.

Working in such a busy shopping area as Kingsmead, you can't help but get to know some of the local people, and you end up talking about different things related to the area. One such tale was that of the sights and sounds of a young girl, who was seen by security guards and heard by staff at the nearby branch of Sainsbury's. She was often seen or heard playing and laughing in the area that was the store's main stockroom, and many of the staff often found it unsettling to be in this area on their own.

My own experience began one day when there was just me and one other employee in the Southern Electric Showroom shop. I had gone up to the first floor to use the toilet, and I had not been in there long when I could hear the sound of a female voice singing in a "la la la" fashion. This sound went right past the bathroom door as though someone had walked past towards the stock room. Concerned that the other member of staff had left the shop unattended (it was company policy never to do this because of the threat of shoplifters) I finished my ablutions and headed towards the stock room. My primary reason was to find out why my colleague had left the store unattended and why she was so happy that she was singing. However, when I reached the stock room there was nobody there to be seen. Feeling slightly perplexed, I went back downstairs in order to ask my assistant whether she had been upstairs, only to find that she was dealing with a long line of customers who were paying their electricity bills, and there was no way that she could have been upstairs when I was in the toilet. In addition to which, there is no way that members of the public could gain access to this part of the building, as the door is always locked and can only be opened with the security code.

On another occasion, I was in the kitchen making tea when from the training room next door I heard the sound of the television. It was that white noise sound you get when your television is on an unturned channel with a snowy screen. Something had caused the television to come on like that, and the volume was also turned up to the maximum. Having gone and turned the television off, I remembered that modern televisions don't normally make that whooshing noise, and turning the set back on I got that blue screen and silence, no static or white noise, nothing. I had done nothing but switch the set off and then back on again, and just to make sure, I repeated it twice more and got exactly the same effect.

However, the most disturbing incident happened one evening, when I had locked up the shop and was in the accounts section, whilst my colleague went to the kitchen to put the kettle on. As I was sat there counting the money and closing the till I happened to look up and across the showroom floor, and there in front of me I could see an elderly gent in a long beige raincoat and cloth cap. He had greying or white hair and was sporting a pair of dark rimmed spectacles, and he was looking at one of the electric cookers we have on display in the showroom. He was literally about 10 feet away from where I was sitting, and so could see him very clearly, and I can still picture him clearly to this day.

Thinking that I had inadvertently locked someone in the shop, I called out to ask him if he needed any help, but I received no reply. Concluding that the poor guy was a bit deaf I got up from my chair and headed into the showroom. However, by the time I got there he was nowhere to be seen, and the place was locked up tight, with no other means of egress.

After I told my colleagues what I had seen I did come in for some light hearted ribbing, but it is true to say that no one enjoyed being left alone in the shop even before I told them about my experiences, so they must have sensed something.

A while later I had the good fortune to be promoted and transferred to a store in Haslemere where I was to become the new manager. After a few months working there I received a phone call, totally out of the blue, from one of my ex-colleagues at Farnborough. She described how she had just seen the old man who I described, standing in the exact same place and wearing the exact same clothes. The shop was all locked up and she couldn't explain it either.

Southern Electric shut all of their shops eventually, and the site of this one particular store in the Kingsmead Shopping Centre was later to become a hairdressers. Nevertheless, the spooky shenanigans continued with the new tenants. Footsteps have been heard ascending and descending the stairs, whilst some employees have reported being tripped up on the second flight of stairs.

Since the recent redevelopment, it is hard to ascertain which store is now on the site of the former Southern Electric shop and subsequent hair dressing salon, and whether the old man and the girl have found a new host for their visits.

Farnborough town centre

Fleet

<u>The White Lady of Bagwell Lane</u>

Bagwell Lane is situated between the towns of Fleet and Hook in the northern part of the county. It is a narrow country lane that is in an area that is sparsely populated, however, there seems to be one resident who is not of this Earth. The spook in question is said to be the returning spirit of a young woman who committed suicide in one of the many ponds in the area around Bagwell Lane. She appears without warning to passing motorists before gliding through the hedgerows and vanishing into a pond.

On one occasion three people witnessed a woman wearing a white dress or gown, she glided across the fields and disappeared beneath the waters of a pond, yet despite appearing to go beneath the surface of the water, the water itself was not disturbed.

Another witness was a lone motorcyclist who happened to be travelling along Bagwell Lane one spring evening in 1968. His journey had been uneventful until halfway along the lane he encountered a ghostly figure dressed in white who appeared in front of him, causing him to brake hard and almost lose control. After coming to a halt and regaining his composure, he turned around to discover the same woman standing in the middle of the road. Unnerved by this experience, the man quickly set off for home, not stopping to look back!

A cyclist who witnessed the white lady described how she appeared and disappeared in an instant, yet in the short time he had seen her, he noticed that her face was wet and carrying a forlorn expression. In addition to which, her clothes and hair seemed to be of another time entirely.

Gosport

Fort Brockhurst

Fort Brockhurst is one of a number of similar fortifications that were designed and built in the mid 19th century in order to protect the city of Portsmouth and the South Coast from invasion. These days the site is owned by English Heritage, and visitors can get a feel of what life was like back in the forts heyday. However, there is one visitor who seems to be unable or unwilling to leave, and popular opinion is that it is the spirit of a sergeant who can still be heard walking along the corridors, whistling out of tune, something that he no doubt did on a regular basis when alive.

Priddy's Hard

Now home to the Explosion Museum of Naval Firepower, Priddy's Hard was once the site of an armament depot, and its history is littered with the death and disease of the people who used to live and work there. Being an armament depot, the handling of high explosives was a regular occurrence and there were many accidents. One such incident involved the accidental detonation of explosives that killed a worker known as Edward George McBride, who was gruesomely torn apart by the force of the explosion. Now it is said that the blood stain of what was left of poor Edward after the explosion, often reappears on the wall of the room which now occupies the site of his untimely demise.

The Royal Hospital Haslar

A Gosport landmark for more than 250 years, the Royal Hospital Haslar sits on the seafront, where it played a major role in the treatment and recuperation of military personnel. Sadly, the hospital lost its military status in 2007, and is now closed. However, a lot of the structures are now Grade II listed, meaning that these elegant buildings are safe from the developers wrecking ball.

As with many historical hospitals, Haslar hospital is home to a number of reported hauntings, and many people have reported strange and unexplained occurrences in several locations within the hospital grounds. Starting in the Galley area, there are said to be three ghosts that have been encountered in one form or another through the years.

For the most part, the hauntings that have taken place in this part of the hospital include cutlery being thrown around, taps being turned on by an unseen hand, and the files in the office being tipped over the floor on several occasions. One of the ghosts obviously does not like loud noises, as the radio that the staff used to listen to whilst working would have its volume mysteriously turned down even when nobody was anywhere near it. However, it is not just poltergeist activity that has been witnessed in the Galley area, as many witnesses have said that they have encountered the ghosts of a man and an old woman at various times. On one occasion, one of the wardroom stewards encountered an old woman coming down the spiral staircase as she was ascending. Thinking that the old woman was lost, the steward enquired whether she needed any help, but instead of receiving a reply, the woman just vanished.

On another occasion, the image of a man has been seen in the corridor outside of the Galley, and one staff member saw a man looking through the glass panel in the door. Thinking that the man needed assistance, the staff member went to investigate, but when they opened the door, there was nobody there. This corridor has also been reported as being bitterly cold, even on the hottest days of the year, or when the heating has been on during the colder months and the rest of the area is warm. Unsettlingly, the Galley and its cold corridor were located opposite F Block, which used to house the lunatic asylum, and many psychics claim that this area is a hotspot for psychic activity.

Another location where people have had strange experiences is in and around the corridors that lead to the operating theatres, where it was not unusual for staff members to feel as though they were being followed. Other people often felt a strong sense of fear and dread when visiting the area, and disembodied footsteps have often been heard, with many people admitting that they have quickened their step when walking the corridors. In fact, so spooked were some members of staff that many of them would rather take a longer walk from B Block to E Block in order to avoid those particular corridors.

The former children's ward in D Block is also said to be haunted, and the ghost of a young girl has been seen running around the top floor. Apparently, many children were killed in a fire in this area, although details of this tragedy remain elusive.

Finally, two other areas of the hospital were also said to be haunted, and these are the cellars, which were originally used as operating theatres and then to house the insane, and the Canada block, which got its name as it was built by the money raised by the "Women of Canada" during World War I. In the cellars, it is said that you can still hear the rattling of chains and the screams of the injured and the insane. Whilst the Canada Block is said to be the home of the ghost of a nurse who hanged herself during the Great War.

The entrance to the Royal Hospital, Haslar

Hayling Island

The Ghost of Hayling Island Station

Hayling Island is a small island that is situated just south of Havant and is connected to the mainland by a bridge to the north, with a ferry service to Portsea giving access to nearby Portsmouth. Hayling Island also used to have a railway, which became affectionately known as Hayling Billy, a name which persists to this day even though the line has long been torn up. The name now relates to a footpath and trail that follows the route of the old line between the village of Langstone on the mainland and the site of Hayling Island station, which is now a theatre.

The line was opened in 1865, primarily for goods traffic, however, two years later the first passenger trains arrived, as the area became popular with holidaymakers. This popularity often meant that the carriages would be jammed packed with travellers in the summer months, but those same carriages would be all but empty during the winter. This meant that the line often struggled to make a profit. Nevertheless, at the time of its closure, the line was actually making a small profit, but the old wooden bridge that linked the island to the mainland was in urgent need of repair. With the cost of replacing or repairing the bridge being seen as too expensive and with passenger numbers falling away, it was decided in 1963 to close the line for good. It wasn't long before most of the line and buildings were either taken-up or demolished completely, before all that remained was the goods shed and the platform at Hayling station.

As the years went by and dereliction set into the remnants of this once thriving tourist line, the Hayling Billy line became nothing more than a distant memory for most local people. However, for some people the memories of the Hayling Billy line would carry on in a peculiar way.

The first report of unusual occurrences came in 1969, a mere six years after the closure of the line. It was a Havant council workman and a fitter employed by the Southern Electricity Board who first encountered a ghost at the old station. Both men were completing routine jobs on the site, and one of the men reported that he had turned around whilst crouching down, only to see a pair of legs behind him. As he attempted to stand up, the figure, which had been wearing black boots and faded trousers, had completely vanished. Later on in the late 1970's, another council workman, Peter Warden, was working at his desk when all of a sudden something grabbed his arm, causing him to jump to his feet, yet there was nothing there.

Another man, who just happened to be walking his dog along the footpath that followed the course of the old railway line, also had an interesting experience near to the station. He wandered around the station building, which by then was falling into serious decay, thinking about how great the place must have been in its heyday. Yet, when he tried to get his dog to move closer to the station building it point-blank refused, and he noticed that the dog's hair was standing on end and the animal was clearly in a state of distress. The man had never seen his dog behave in this way before, and after a second unsuccessful attempt at getting the dog to enter the station building, he dropped the lead and headed inside alone. Inside he witnessed nothing other than the decay associated with an abandoned ticket office, and eventually, the man left with his dog only too eager to leave the place behind. When he arrived home the man related the story of his experiences to his father-in-law. That is when he was told that that was the room where the station master died. It seems as though the old station master was so connected to the building that he was not keen on leaving it.

In the end, it was the goods shed that was the only part of the site still in a usable condition, and the shed was often used by Havant and Waterlooville council for storage purposes. In due course, the building was purchased by the Hayling Island Amateur Dramatics Society, and converted into a 144 seat theatre. Yet, even now there are stories of people involved in the theatre feeling uncomfortable when locking up late at night, and some people have heard heavy breathing and footsteps in the auditorium, when there has been nobody there.

St. Peter's Church

One of the island's churches is said to be haunted, with the ghost of a sailor often being seen within St. Peter's church. The story goes that at a time when the only connection to the island was via a causeway, a local girl was waiting patiently for her sailor boyfriend in the church as they had arranged previously. However, he failed to show up, and it transpired that in his haste to get to his rendezvous he crossed the causeway at the wrong time and was swept to his death by the tide. Only his spirit made it to the church it seems, and he has often been seen sitting at the back of the church waiting for his girlfriend.

Old Fleet Manor

One of the oldest (and some say the oddest) house on the island is Old Fleet Manor, and it comes as no surprise that this 15th century listed building is home to its very own ghostly presence, known as the man in black. This ancient dwelling was originally a farmhouse, and it has everything that you would expect from a building constructed in the 15th century, low ceilings, old beams, and staircases so cramped and narrow, that the only way to get a coffin downstairs was via a trapdoor in the floor, known as a 'coffin-drop'. It is the room where this trapdoor is situated where some people have experienced the rather unsettling sensation of having their brow and hair stroked by unseen fingers. The figure known as the man in black was often seen or sensed by both people and animals in the house, and it was not uncommon for the owner's dogs and cats to stand aside as if letting some unseen figure walk past them.

Hinton Ampner

The Grey Man of Hinton Ampner House

Now owned by the National Trust, Hinton Ampner House is now more well-known for its spectacular gardens than for the house itself, although it is home to some fine paintings. However, the original Hinton Ampner House was more infamous for the hauntings and disturbances that took place there during the 18th century.

The account of the disturbances that gripped Hinton Ampner was first set down by Mary Ricketts, who, with her children, servants, and her brother, witnessed manifestations of a most eerie and frightening sort. Ricketts was intelligent and widely read and her reputation for truthfulness forever went unsullied. Her brother, John Jervis, was named Baron Jervis and Earl St. Vincent for his distinguished naval services. The Hinton Ampner case was published in the Journal of the Society for Psychical Research in April 1893, and is reproduced in full here:-

In 1757, Mary had married William Henry Ricketts of Canaan, Jamaica, and they moved into the large country home outside of Hinton Ampner, England. From the very first there had been disturbances, the sound of doors slamming, the shuffling of footsteps. Ricketts had spent many nights watching for the "prowlers" that he was convinced had somehow gained entrance into the house. They had lived there for about six months when their nurse swore that she saw a gentleman in a drab-coloured suit of clothes go into the yellow room. Such things as these the Ricketts tolerated for four years, firmly convinced that the noises were the result of wind and prowlers, and that the gray man and a once-sighted figure of a woman were the products of the servant's imagination.

For several years, Mary Ricketts accompanied her husband on his frequent business trips to the West Indies, but, in 1769, having now mothered three children she decided to remain alone in England at the old manor house that they occupied. Because they were convinced of a natural explanation for the disturbances, William had no pronounced anxiety when Mary told him that she felt that she should remain in England with the children while he made the trip to Jamaica. After all, she did have eight servants to assist her, and it was quite unlikely that any prowler would try to take on such odds.

The phenomena seemed almost to have been waiting for William Ricketts to leave on an extended trip before it began its manifestations in earnest. He had only been gone a short time when, one afternoon while lying down in her room, Mary heard the noise of someone walking in the room and the rustling of silk clothing as it brushed the floor. She opened her eyes to see absolutely no one. She called the servants and a thorough search was made of the upstairs rooms and closets. The cook reminded her mistress that she had heard the same rustling noise descending the stairs on several occasions and had once seen the tall figure of a woman in dark clothes. Ricketts found herself being less dismissive of the servants' stories now that she, too, had heard the spectral rustling of an invisible lady.

Nocturnal noises continued, and, one night, as Mary Ricketts lay sleeping in the yellow room which the "grey man" had been seen to enter, she was awakened by the heavy plodding steps of a man walking toward the foot of her bed. She was too frightened to reach for the bell at her bedside. She jumped from her bed and ran from the room into the nursery. The children's nurse was instantly out of her bed, rubbing her sleep-swollen eyes and wondering what on earth had so upset the mistress of the house. The nurse became immediately awake when Mary Ricketts told her about the heavy footsteps. The rest of the servants were summoned and again a fruitless search was made to discover some human agency who might be responsible for the disturbance.

It was in November that the knocking and rapping's begun. A few months later, after the first of the year, Mary Ricketts and her household noticed that the entire house seemed to be filled with the sound of a "hollow murmuring." A maid, who had spent the night in the yellow room, appeared at the breakfast table pale faced and shaken over the dismal groans that she had heard around her bed most of the night.

By midsummer the eerie sound of voices in the night had become intolerable. They began before the household went to bed, and with brief intermissions were heard until after broad day in the morning. Mary Ricketts could frequently distinguish articulate sounds. Usually a shrill female voice would begin, and then two others with deeper and manlike tones joined in the discourse. Although the conversation often sounded as if it were taking place close to her, she never could distinguish actual words.

At last, Mary Ricketts appealed to her brother, the Earl St. Vincent, to come to her aid. Earlier, he had spent a few days at Hinton Ampner and had heard nothing, but now the urgency in his sister's letter convinced him that whatever was troubling her was real—at least to her and the servants. When the Earl St. Vincent arrived at the mansion, he had in his company a well-armed manservant. The earl was convinced that some disrespectful pranksters had conspired to annoy his sister and her household, and he was determined to deal out swift justice. Captain Luttrell, a neighbour of the Ricketts, joined in this campaign to exorcise the spooks. Captain Luttrell was familiar with the old legends of the area and had accepted the possibility of a supernatural agency at work, but he had volunteered his services to determine the cause of the disturbances, regardless of their origin.

The three armed men were kept on the go all night by the sound of doors opening and slamming. Mary Ricketts's brother became a believer in the world unseen. He soon concluded that the disturbances were definitely not the results of any human activity. Captain Luttrell declared that Hinton Ampner was unfit for human occupancy and urged Mary Ricketts to move out at once.

The Earl St. Vincent agreed with his sister's neighbour, but he realized that she could not quit the house so easily. She needed a certain amount of time to notify her husband and landlord of her decision, and the necessary preparations had to be made to obtain a different house. He told Mary that he would stand guard every night for a week, sleeping by day and watching by night.

The brother had maintained his vigil for about three nights when Mary was awakened by the sound of a pistol shot and the groans of a person in mortal agony. She was too frightened to move, but she felt secure in the knowledge that her brother and his servant were quite capable of handling any monster.

When her brother awoke the next afternoon, Mary quickly questioned him about the struggle that she heard the night before. The Earl St. Vincent frowned and shook his head in disbelief. He had heard neither shot nor any of the terrible groaning.

The earl himself was forced to experience the frustration of hearing sounds that no one else could perceive on the next day. He was lying in his bed, having just awakened from his afternoon's sleep, when he heard a sound as if an immense weight had fallen through the ceiling to the floor. He leaped out of bed, fully expecting to see a gaping hole in both ceiling and floor. There was not the slightest splinter, nor had anyone else in the mansion heard the crash. Even his servant, who slept in the bedroom directly below, had heard nothing.

The earl insisted that his sister leave at once, and, because he was unable to stay at Hinton Ampner any longer, he ordered his Lieutenant of Marines to the mansion to assist Mary in her moving chores and to maintain the nightly watch. Mary Ricketts gave notice to her landlord, Lady Hillsborough, and immediately set the servants to work packing trunks and bags. The night after her brother left, she and the entire household heard a crash such as the one that he had described. The crash was followed by several piercing shrieks, dying away as though sinking into the earth.

To disguise her fear, the nurse flippantly remarked how pleasant the sound was and how she would love to hear more noises such as that. The unfortunate woman was troubled with horrid screaming and groaning in her room every night until the household moved.

Mary Ricketts returned to Hinton Ampner only once after she had moved away. She entered the house alone and heard a sound that she had never heard before, a sound that she said caused her "indescribable terror."

Lady Hillsborough sent her agent, a Mr. Sainsbury, to stay a night in the house and to test the truth of the rumours about her manor. Mr. Sainsbury did not last the night.

In 1772, a family named Lawrence moved into Hinton Ampner. Their servants reported seeing an apparition of a woman, but the Lawrence's threatened their servants not to make any statements. They lasted a year before they moved out. After their occupancy, the house was pulled down to be used in the construction of a new manor.

When Mary Ricketts resided in the mansion, an old man had come to her with a tale about having boarded up a small container for Lord Stawell, the original owner of Hinton Ampner. He had suggested that the small box might have contained treasure and might offer a clue to the haunting. Workmen discovered the container when they were stripping the mansion. It was found to conceal the skeleton of a baby.

When Mary Ricketts learned of this startling discovery, it seemed to offer the final key to the legend of Hinton Ampner. The villagers said Lord Stawell had engaged in illicit relations with the younger sister of his wife, who had lived with them at the manor. It had been the subject of ancient gossip that his sister-in-law had borne his child—a child that had been murdered at its birth. When Lady Stawell died, her sister, Honoria, became the mistress of Hinton Ampner. The past wrongs began to form a chain of evil: The first Lady Stawell, wronged by a younger sister and an indiscreet husband; the innocent babe, born of an illicit union, murdered, its body boarded up in the walls of the manor. Lord Stawell, the perpetrator of most of the sins, was himself left on his bed in the yellow room to die in agony, while his family waited outside, ignoring his groans of pain.

It was shortly after Lord Stawell's death in 1755 that the groom swore that his old master had appeared to him in his room. The groom knew that it was the master because of the drab-coloured gray clothing that Lord Stawell was so fond of wearing. From that time on, the "grey man" and his groans and plodding footsteps were heard in the corridors of Hinton Ampner. The lady was said to have been the phantom of the first Lady Stawell.

Hinton Ampner House

Photo: Rwendland

Lymington

The Angel Inn

One of the oldest pubs in Lymington, a recent refurbishment has seen the pubs name changed to the rather unfortunate, Angel and Blue Pig. Trendy new name aside, this particular establishment dates back to the 13th century, and it claims to be one of the most haunted pubs not only in Hampshire, but in Britain.

It is said that the pub is home to two or three ghosts, with the most famous and most sighted spook being that of a phantom coachman. He is often seen in the first light of the morning, his nose pressed up against the window of the pubs kitchen. The inn was often frequented by coachmen, who tired from their journey along the rough lanes of the New Forest, would stay here for some much needed rest and provisions. Nevertheless, no one seems to know why this phantom coachman keeps this early morning vigil, and there are no clues as to his identity either.

Lymington has a long maritime history, and it once rivalled nearby Southampton as a port, and shipbuilding has a long and illustrious history in the town. This may then account for the ghost of a seafarer who has also been seen within the confines of this pub. This spectre is often seen wearing a long naval coat, brass buttons and all, which is fastened to the neck.

There have also been reports of a third apparition, a young girl in a white dress with long shoulder length hair, and she has been seen on more than one occasion on the second floor, but no one seems to know the story of this particular haunting.

Maybe this phantom girl was responsible for the ghostly occurrence that took place one night back in 1966, the playing of a phantom piano. During this time, the pub was under the management of a Mr.

McKinley, and one day his brother and sister-in-law were visiting and had agreed to stay the night at the pub. Having left the two brothers chatting at the bar, the lady in question took herself off to bed, but her plans to get a good night's sleep were disturbed by the noise of a piano being played in the next room. When the manager came upstairs he was confronted by his rather annoyed sister-in-law, who took him to task over the playing of a piano at that time of night.

Despite the man's insistence that the room in question was empty (it was an assembly hall) the woman refused to believe that she had been mistaken. In order to prove his point, Mr. McKinley unlocked the room in order to show his sister-in-law that there was indeed no piano, or for that matter, anything else in the room that could have made a noise. Yet, the chilling twist comes from the fact that the room had been home to a piano, which had been battered and beyond use for many years, but had only just been removed and scrapped the day before.

The Angel Inn, now the Angel and Blue Pig

Middle Wallop

The Museum of Army Flying

Middle Wallop airfield played a pivotal role in the fight against Nazi Germany during World War 2, and as a consequence it was bombed on a regular basis during the Battle of Britain. With plenty of history attached to the place, as well as several World War 2 buildings still on site, it comes as no surprise to find that the place has been the home to a number of ghostly sightings over the years. The museum itself is supposedly haunted by the ghosts of three workers who were killed when a hanger exploded during an air raid and one of the hefty hangar doors subsequently fell on them. In addition to this, a WAAF who was also killed during the same raid is often seen still riding her bicycle in a frantic but ultimately futile attempt to escape death.

Middle Wallop airfield and Museum of Army Flying

Photo: Peter Facey

Portsmouth & Southsea

Wymering Manor

Many places claim to be the most haunted house in Britain without much foundation, even so, Wymering Manor in Portsmouth must surely be in contention for the title, as it is said to be home to anywhere between 20 and 30 ghosts.

Most of the current structure dates back to the 16th century, however, there has been a house on this site going back as far as 1042, and it is mentioned in the Doomsday Book. Despite being rebuilt and remodelled through the centuries, some of the materials from the medieval era can still be seen today, and it now has Grade II listed status.

The house has a rich history, and it has been owned by countless numbers of people, as well as the local authority through the centuries, and due to its colourful history, it is now said to be one of the most haunted houses in the country. So, let us take a closer look at some of the more popular hauntings that are associated with this ancient property.

One of the most well known hauntings is said to be a choir of nuns. These apparitions were first seen by a Mr. Metcalf, who used to see the nuns walking across the manor's hall at midnight, chanting as they went. It is said that this ghostly congregation is the reappearance of nuns from the Sisterhood of Saint Mary the Virgin, who stayed at the house during the 1800s.

Ghostly unseen hands have also been at work in the building, especially in the room known as the 'Panelled Room'. Many people have reported that they have felt a hand touch them on the head or shoulders, whilst other people have felt an oppressive atmosphere in the room, and they refuse to stay in it for long periods of time. Even today, many people often say that they are overcome with a sudden

feeling of fear or an inexplicable feeling that they need to flee the room quickly. When the house was closed, many security guards refused to enter the building alone, and they would make a point of not going too close to the Panelled Room.

Other hauntings include the sound of children either whispering or laughing, and then there is the tale of Reckless Roddy. This story dates back to the Middle-Ages when a couple of newlyweds came to stay at the manor house, and the husband was rather unfortunately called away suddenly on urgent business. Hearing that a new bride was staying alone in the property, local lothario Sir Roderick of Portchester, set about trying to woo the woman whilst her husband was away. Unfortunately, at least from Reckless Roddy's point of view, the husband arrived back sooner than expected, and finding Roddy in mid-seduction, chased him from the house, catching him as he attempted to mount his horse in the courtyard, and make good his escape. However, the irate husband killed Reckless Roddy before he could get away, and legend has it that any newlyweds who stay at the house can often hear the galloping footsteps of Reckless Roddy's horse running away from the building.

Droxford House

Unlike Wymering Manor, Droxford House is a building that consists of apartments owned by the local council, yet there have been a number of reports of strange goings-on in some of the flats by those living there. More often than not, local councils can be more than a little bit sceptical of reports from their tenants about haunted homes, as it could just be a way in which to secure a move to another property. Nevertheless, there has been more than one report of unexplained phenomena, and from various tenants through the years. Built in 1957, Droxford House replaced a row of dilapidated terraced houses, but it seems that some of the tenants who were displaced from their homes to make way for the new construction were not too happy about it.

Everything seemed fine at first, and it wasn't until late 1987 that the first reports of strange occurrences began being reported, firstly by a

Mrs. Maltby, and then by other tenants as well. Mrs. Maltby had not long moved in to her flat in Droxford House with her baby daughter, when strange things began to occur. There were unexplained knocking sounds, there were loud noises on the 4th step on the stairs, and her daughter's toys would mysteriously be moved. As time went on the disturbances became more intense, and she began to notice a faint shadow at the top of the stairs. However, the apparitions would go stronger, and she even claimed to have seen the ghostly figure of a black man with grey hair and aged in his early 50's, who climbed into her bed.

Despite claims that she was inventing stories in order to engineer a move to another property, Mrs. Maltby insisted that she was happy in her home, and she did not want to move as she was close to her friends and family. It wasn't until two council wardens visited her property that her claims of her flat being haunted received extra credence. During their visit the wardens witnessed the playing of an electric organ in the flat, despite the fact that it was not plugged in and had no batteries in it. In fact, so unnerved was one of the wardens that they stated that they would never set foot inside her home ever again.

Eventually, after enduring 10 months of hauntings Mrs. Maltby employed the services of a local priest who performed an exorcism, which seemed to put an end to the hauntings in her flat at least, however, for other residents it was a different matter.

During February 1990, additional spooky shenanigans began to be reported by tenants living on the second floor of the building. One female resident discovered her pullover being tugged by an unseen hand when sitting alone, whilst her grand-daughter stated that she had seen an old man in the bathroom. Another tenant would often hear footsteps on the stairs despite being alone in the flat, and on two occasions her fridge-freezer had been switched off, even though the plug socket was out of reach of her 3 year old son. In addition to that, her son reported seeing faces in the bathroom, and the mobile hanging in her son's room would often swing around despite the air being completely still. Intrigued by these occurrences the tenant contacted the previous resident of her flat, only to be told that they too had been spooked by the sudden appearance of a man in a grey suit in the bathroom. A local medium was called in, and she said that the spirit was of a man called Mr. Mullen, who had lived in one of the houses that had been demolished to make way for the construction of Droxford House.

The Theatre Royal

This Grade II listed building has had a long history, and not all of it illustrious. It has been left to decay, been severely damaged by fire, and has been scheduled for demolition on more than one occasion. However, to their credit, the people of Portsmouth have refused to let this theatre vanish from the landscape.

The theatre was the scene of a particularly gruesome suicide of an actor, who is said to have slit his own throat sometime during the 1880s, and now his wraith has been seen skulking about at the back of the theatre on more than one occasion down the years. Many people have heard ghostly footsteps, and plenty of actors and stage hands have commented on how they have felt a presence whilst standing in the wings, including an actress who was shoved towards the stage whilst waiting for her cue. When the woman turned around there was nobody to be seen.

The Haunted Pubs of Portsmouth

Next door to the Theatre Royal lies the White Swan public house, which is said to be host to the spirit of a serving wench who was brutally murdered by her sailor husband back sometime in the 1880s. The story goes that whilst her husband was away in service of his country, this barmaid succumbed to the lecherous attentions of more than one of the pubs patrons. Upon the sailors return, an argument ensued and the unfaithful barmaid was slain by her irate husband in front of the hearth. Now her spirit is often seen walking near to the spot where her life ended.

Two of the cities hostelries claim to be the home of the spirit of the great wartime diver Lionel 'Buster' Crabb, who disappeared in mysterious circumstances whilst diving in Portsmouth Harbour. His mission was to investigate a Soviet cruiser that was docked in the port, but he never returned, and a body missing its head and hands was later discovered floating in Chichester Harbour wearing his diving suit. Now, both the Sally Port Hotel and the nearby Kepples Head Hotel both claim that they are now the site of Buster Crabb's ghost, as they were said to be his last port of call for the night before his mission.

Fort Widley

During the 1800s the biggest fear was an invasion by forces from France, and this prompted the then Prime Minister, Lord Palmerston to call for a review of the defences along the south coast and especially Portsmouth. During 1861, Fort Widley became part of the defences situated along the length of Portsdown Hill, which quickly became dubbed as 'Palmerston's Folly', as it soon became apparent that the threat of invasion from France was over estimated.

The fort is a massive structure, and it consists of a number of subterranean rooms and tunnels that were big enough to accommodate up to 250 men. The fort was one of six that was built, but by the time they were all completed the threat from France had diminished. That being said, the fort, its rooms and tunnels did see action during World War II as planning rooms and to house the Bomb Disposal Unit of the Royal Engineers. In addition to which, it was also used to house prisoners of war from 1942, and it would have been used as an emergency administrative centre in the case of a nuclear war, which lasted until the end of the cold war in the early 1990s.

It is the underground tunnels and rooms that are said to be haunted, and some of the many ghostly residents include the spirit of a sergeant-major who likes to whistle whilst haunting the building. The fort's keep is another location where ghostly footsteps and knockings have been heard, which are said to be made by a former prison guard or prisoner.

The ghost of a small boy has often been seen in the labyrinth of tunnels under the fort, and the story goes that it is the spirit of a drummer boy, who fell to his death down a spiral staircase after being chased by a superior officer after being disobedient. His footsteps have been heard running along the tunnels, and he sometimes plays games.

Southsea Castle

Another location that has many underground rooms and tunnels that are said to be haunted is Southsea Castle. As with Fort Widley, the castle was built as part of a wider scheme to protect the south coast of England from invasion by France or Spain, during the time of Henry VIII. The castle has had many uses, including as a lighthouse and as a military prison during Victorian times, before being retired from military service in 1960.

Hauntings are said to include the sight of a ghostly lady in white, whose identity is not known, and during several ghost hunting expeditions, a number of investigators have been pushed or shoved by some unseen force.

The Old Beneficiary School

Now home to the Groundlings Theatre, The Old Beneficiary School in Portsea is said to be one of the most haunted locations in Portsmouth. It is still affectionately known as 'The Old Benny' and it is a Grade II listed building which was built in Georgian times for the specific purposes of providing poor children (specifically boys, but later girls were admitted) with an education. Needless to say, but discipline of the children was harsh and draconian by today's standards, and one of the original features that can still be seen inside the building is a hook that children were tied to when receiving the birch. The reported activity in this building includes the sounds of children laughing and playing, whilst the ghost of a boy (nicknamed 'little George') has been witnessed by several people sitting on the stairs, whilst the ghost of a little girl (known as Emily) has been seen in one of the former classrooms. There have also been numerous reports of poltergeist activity, and cold spots located in the building even on hot days. There is also a strong smell of lavender in one of the downstairs rooms that has no explanation.

Southsea Castle

Photo: Geni

Romsey

The Palmerston Bakery and Restaurant

The market town of Romsey has a long and colourful history, and thanks to its long and ancient origins, there have been a number of reports of spooky goings-on in the area. There used to be a bakery and restaurant in Market Place called The Palmerston, and it was said to be haunted by a ghost that became known as "Charlie". Despite the nickname, staff at the bakery never enjoyed Charlie's visits, and many of them were too afraid to climb the narrow and claustrophobic staircase to the attic. Charlie's presence has been felt both in the attic and in a boiler room below, and many staff refused to go near the attic. Charlie's manifestations consisted of more than just strange noises, lights were said to have turned themselves on and off, and toilets have flushed despite the bathroom being empty. On one occasion, some staff and the manageress were alone in the restaurant when they were almost frightened out of their wits by a large bang coming from one of the upstairs rooms. So terrified were they that they all fled in sheer terror, rather than investigate the origins of the noise. On another occasion, a man living in the neighbouring flat was witness to a succession of loud noises coming from The Palmerston late one night. Concerned that the premises may have been broken into, he called the police, who, on inspection, discovered no signs of a break in or any other reason for the noise.

The Old Swan Inn

This public house has now been converted in to a Conservative Club, however, the legend of the two dead Roundhead soldiers lives on. The story relates to the period of the English Civil War, with the town of Romsey very much on the side of the Royalists. Two of Cromwell's soldiers were captured and hanged, the ropes being slung over a metal sign outside the pub. Legend has it that one of the soldiers managed to get extricate himself from his predicament and make good his escape. Unfortunately, the soldier's good fortune was not too last, and he died of his injuries in the alley next to the pub. Now it is said that you can still here the screams of the two men in their death throes.

Above: The Old Swan Inn, Romsey
Below: The sign post where the two Roundheads were allegedly put to death

Southampton

Netley Abbey & Netley Military Hospital

On the outskirts of Southampton lies the village of Netley, which is famous for two important historical landmarks. The first, Netley Abbey, was built in 1239 and despite not producing anyone of note, it became well known and respected for the hospitality and help that its inhabitants offered to weary travellers and the needy. When Henry VIII dissolved the monasteries in 1536 the abbey was converted into a mansion, which it remained for the next 175 years or so, before eventually becoming derelict and pilfered for building materials. Now it lies in ruins, and despite the fact that no Earthly creatures now call this ancient building home, it is said that the site is home to at least two ghosts. The first is said to be the ghost of an abbot, who appears as a dark figure, and the second is a monk who appears as a white figure. It is also said that if you listen carefully on a still night, you can just make out the sound of ghostly chanting.

The second famous landmark in the area was the Netley Military Hospital, which was an impressively large structure that would be home to a vast number of injured UK and Commonwealth soldiers from a number of different wars. Even by the standards of the day the hospital was an imposing building, and it could accommodate as many as 1,400 patients in its 180 wards. These wards were spread out among the structure's long and wide corridors, which stretched for 200 yards on each side of the central chapel, and across three floors.

The haunting associated with the hospital is the apparition of the 'Grey Lady', who has been seen and heard on a number of occasions down the years. One of the first sightings of the phantom nurse was in 1878, and she has been seen many times since, and reports of sightings persist today, even though only the chapel remains from the original building. The story behind the Grey Lady could just be folklore, but the story goes that a nurse who began a relationship with a patient, committed suicide through guilt after administering poison to her lover, after she found him in the arms of another nurse. However, another version of this story is eerily similar to the story of the Grey Lady of the Cambridge Military Hospital (see Aldershot), where the nurse committed suicide after accidently killing the patient after administering a fatal overdose of medication. No matter what the story surrounding her death, there has been no shortage of sightings of the phantom nurse. She was sighted most often on the ground floor, in and around the main corridor, and night workers were those people who were most likely to encounter this restless spirit.

By the late fifties the building had become largely surplus to requirements, and eventually it was closed. Unfortunately, this magnificent building was earmarked for demolition, and the demolition process began during 1966. So strong was the legend of the Grey Lady that many big and burly workmen were spooked enough to refuse to work on the site. Eventually, some reporters and psychic investigators decided to visit the site in order to try and capture evidence of the existence of the ghostly nurse before the building was lost for good. They explored what was left of the south wing and the centre without success, but their luck changed when they walked past the entrance to Ward 27. It was here that all four men saw what looked to be a woman in an old fashioned grey nurse's uniform. So scared were they that they hastily made their egress from the building via a broken window! One of the group decided to re-enter the building to see if they had been the victims of a hoax, but all four of

The imposing Netley Military Hospital

the men maintained that what they had seen was totally genuine.

Once the final parts of the hospital were demolished and cleared away, the site was given over to parkland, with only the central chapel remaining in use as a visitor centre. Nevertheless, the tale of the Grey Lady of Netley Hospital remains to this day, and there are still the odd sighting being reported of her in the grounds of what is now Royal Victoria Country Park.

Effy, the ghost of Southampton Eye Hospital

Another ghost associated with a hospital in Southampton is Effy. This name was given to the spirit by workers at the old Southampton Eye Hospital site on the corner of Wilton Avenue and Bedford Place. This spirit was seen by both patients and workers alike, wandering through the corridors and wards of the hospital. The story behind this particular ghost is that "Effy", had been a housekeeper when the site was a rectory back in the 19th century, and that she murdered a young

housemaid who she caught in flagrante delicto with her butler boyfriend.

Those who encountered the apparition described Effy as being middle-aged, dressed in grey, wearing an eyeglass that is on a velvet ribbon around her neck.

The building was demolished in 1994, after the eye hospital unit was moved to a new building within the grounds of Southampton General Hospital, and no one knows if Effy now haunts the new buildings on the site.

Avenue Campus

The Avenue Campus is part of the vast Southampton University Campus, and during daylight hours it is bustling with hundreds of students, lecturers and other university staff. However, it is when the sun goes down and all the students have gone that the site becomes host to some unsettling goings-on.

A security guard has stated that he has heard footsteps running along one of the corridors on the first floor. These occurrences usually begin around 1AM, when the security guard is sat in his usual position in the reception area. The area in question is part of the older part of the building, which was originally owned by Taunton's College, and during the war was even used as a hospital for a time. The story of the nurse who accidentally kills a patient by giving them too much medication is one that has cropped up twice already, at both the Cambridge Military Hospital, and the Netley Military Hospital, and it appears that this building is no exception. It is said that a distraught nurse committed suicide after killing a patient by giving him too much morphine, and now many people believe that it is her spirit that can be heard and felt around the site. It is true that many security staff have refused to work in this part of the campus, and in addition to the sound of someone running, there has been reports of doors closing on their own, and the sounds of furniture being moved around, especially in seminar room 1113 in the South corridor.

South Western House

Originally called the South Western Hotel, this building was built in the 1870's to cater for the needs of the wealthy before they boarded one of the many luxurious cruise ships. It was also the last place on land that the well-to-do spent before embarking on the ill-fated maiden voyage of the Titanic in 1912. Nowadays, the building has been converted in to luxury and exclusive apartments, yet there is one resident who has been seen wandering through the corridors of the historic building.

There have been sightings of a man who has been seen in the corridor where room 667 was situated when the building was a hotel. This room was the scene of a botched suicide pact in 1931 between a Mr. Draper and his lover Gladys Tressider. Having shot his lover, Mr. Draper turned the gun on himself, killing him instantly, but little did he know that his companion had not been killed. Now there are sightings of a man who seems to be searching the corridors of the hotel in a frantic state.

There have also been reports of other ghostly happenings, and two security guards were spooked one night whilst doing their rounds at a time when the building had yet been converted into apartments.

Doors to the stairs were heard opening and closing on their own, which the pair put down to draughts, however, later on the lift operated all by itself, despite there being no other people in the building at the time.

Troublesome Tenants

Like most cities of a similar size, Southampton has a number of local authority housing estates at various locations across the city, and some of these homes have been host to unwanted guests of the spectral kind. In the area known as Thornhill, there were a number of unexplained occurrences during the late 1960's and 70's, especially in the Tatwin Crescent area. These blocks of flats were fairly new at the time and it is rumoured that a number of Romany's and travellers were evicted on the site to make way for the new estate, and that so annoyed were they about being moved that they cursed the site and anyone who lived there. So it comes as no surprise that some of the early tenants experienced some rather unsettling happenings, which would usually take place during the winter months. Many residents would dread that time of the year, as more often than not they would be terrorised by a number of unexplained events. These goings-on would include taps being turned full-on, clothes and other possessions being flung across the room, strange voices and mutterings when no one else was in the property and much more besides. One frightened woman told how she noticed a man coming through her front door and walking down the corridor towards the lounge before disappearing. Yet, when she went and checked the front door, it was still locked, just how she left it. So bad was the hauntings and spooky events, and so numerous, that the local council employed the services of a local priest to exorcise the properties, but to no avail, and the hauntings continued. However, there have not been any recent reports of unexplained events, so maybe those restless spirits have found peace at last.

Other locations is Southampton have also been host to some unexplained phenomena, including Canberra Towers in Weston Estate, where I lived for a number of years, and where I and my then wife experienced some unexplained events. Firstly, items would mysteriously disappear for days before suddenly reappearing. One night I was sitting in the living room working on the computer, when I saw a figure out of the corner of my eye pass the doorway and head in to the kitchen. Thinking that my wife had got out of bed I asked her what the matter was, but received no reply. Upon investigating why she had not replied I found the kitchen to be deserted and in darkness, and both my wife and daughter were fast asleep. In addition to which, there was a number of occasions when our daughter would seemingly offer sweets and food to someone who wasn't there. Talking to other people within the block, it emerged that we were not alone in experiencing unsettling and unexplainable events.

Tatwin Crescent, Thornhill

Canberra Towers, Weston

The former Ordnance Survey Headquarters, Romsey Road

Built during the 1960's the then brand new headquarters of the UK's national mapping agency was seen as being state-of-the-art at the time. It was a large site, which was designed to house the 4,000 staff that was employed by the company at the time. Some of the rooms in the buildings were huge, including the print floor and storage areas. Due to developments in technology by the turn of the 21st century, the building had become too large for the ever dwindling number of employees.

In the spring of 2011, Ordnance Survey moved to brand new headquarters on the edge of the city, and the old building was demolished and replaced by housing.

Many people who worked on the site reported strange occurrences and unexplained feelings in certain areas.

One of the most widely reported ghosts was said to be an Irish labourer who was supposed to have been killed during the construction of the site, and it was said that he haunted the corridor that linked the North block to the main William Roy Building.

There were many underground passages that linked the various parts of the buildings together, and many people often reported the sensation of being followed when walking alone along these corridors.

The upper loading bay and copy shop areas also seemed to suffer from unexplainable phenomenon. A large Christmas tree toppled over of its own accord in the copy shop, whilst in the loading bay, a forklift truck started all by itself, doors would open of their own accord, and a strong cold breeze would often flow through the place even though all external doors and windows were shut.

Southampton General Hospital

The site that is now home to Southampton General Hospital was originally occupied by a workhouse, which had been constructed in the early years of the 19th century to house the city's poor. Administered by a group of nuns, the site also included an infirmary to give accommodation and respite care to the sick and elderly. It is during these early years that we find the story of the nurse (or in this case, the nun) who administers the wrong treatment, which results in the death of a patient, and the suicide of the distraught woman. This story has cropped up a number of times including at the Cambridge Military Hospital, and at Netley Military hospital, and it appears again here also.

This is one story that seems to be behind the supposed hauntings of a number of hospitals in the county and one wonders where this incident actually took place, for it seems that its popularity as an explanation for a number of hauntings, means that it is an incident that may well have occurred at some point. I'm sure that there must be a number of other establishments across the country where this story is also connected to alleged hauntings. In this version of the story connected to what is now Southampton General Hospital, the nun, administered the wrong liquid, and her poor patient died a slow and painful death. So distraught was the nun that she committed suicide by swallowing the same liquid, and now her ghost has been seen by a number of the hospitals patients. One such incident was reported in 1972 by a Kathleen Bury, a woman who had been admitted to hospital for treatment for severe head trauma. One morning she awoke to find two figures that appeared to be dressed in some kind of religious habits. As it was first light it was too dark for her to determine who these people were, neither could she determine whether they were male or female. The two mysterious figures made no noise, and feeling slightly ill at ease she rang for the night nurse, but as she did so, the two figures drifted away. Describing the incident to the nurse, she was told that no visitors would have been allowed in at that time in the morning, and that her sighting may well have been connected to the unusual hauntings that have been reported down through the years. In fact, she was told that it was nothing to worry about, and that it was actually a good sign, as these sightings always coincided with patients who went on to make a full recovery, something that Kathleen did and she was discharged a few days later.

The Haunted Pubs of Southampton

The Talking Heads

With a history that stretches back to 1875, the Talking Heads pub in the Portswood area of the city is renowned for being one of the best venues to watch live bands in Southampton. Yet, as well as being a major draw for lovers of live music, the pub is also said to be home to a number of strange occurrences. It is the staff and management that have experienced the lion's share of these strange happenings, and that includes the occasion when the owner was allegedly slapped by an unknown and unseen force. On another occasion, the bar manager claimed that he had seen a mysterious white dress in the corner of his eye in the cellar, and the beer pumps have been switched off when no one had been in the cellar. Both the bar manager and a barmaid were also witnesses to a number of strange noises, and they were both shocked to find that when they asked the "spirit" to make a noise it did so on request.

The Red Lion

One of the oldest public houses in the city, the Red Lion pub is also one of the most haunted, and it has been said that the venue is home to as many as 21 different ghosts, which surely makes this particular pub one of the most haunted in the country. The pub is famous for being the venue where King Henry V held the trial of the three men who conspired to assassinate him. The three men in question

Richard, Earl of Cambridge, Lord Scrope of Masham and Sir Thomas Grey of Heton were all found guilty of trying to kill the King, and they were subsequently hanged for their crime from outside the Bargate. It comes as no surprise then that the ghosts of three men have sometimes been seen leaving the pub together, and maybe it is the spirits of the three traitors making their final, fateful journey to the gallows. Other ghosts that have been seen or heard in the pub include the sighting of four men sitting around the fire enjoying a drink, and a ghostly woman seen behind the bar who is said to be the ghost of a former barmaid who was killed when she fell down the stairs. The ghost of a man in old fashioned clothing has been seen on many occasions, although he is only visible from the knees up due to the adjustment in the height of the floor of the pub over the years.

The Dolphin Hotel

A rival to the Red Lion's claim of being the most haunted pub in Southampton is the Dolphin Hotel. This is an establishment that has been around since the Middle Ages and there are a number of ghosts that are said to frequent the place. The most famous ghost is that of a woman known as "Molly", who has been seen many times throughout the years. Molly was a former chambermaid who fell in love but unfortunately that love was unrequited and the poor girl took her own life in the former stable block.

The Duke of Wellington

It seems as though most of the oldest hostelries in the city seem to have a ghost or two among their clientele, and the Duke of Wellington pub is no exception. It is a venue that is apparently haunted by a spirit who likes to refill the empty glasses of pubs customers. It is said that this particular ale loving spirit is the ghost of an 18 year old who was attacked and press ganged into serving on a merchant vessel. Other ghostly goings-on include fleeting glimpses of shadows in the cellar, an upstairs room that is always icy cold no matter what the outside temperature, as well as items in the bar being moved when there is no one in the vicinity.

Assorted Hauntings

There are a number of other haunted locations to be found around the city and its surrounding suburbs. One such haunted location took place in the area known as Bitterne Manor, where a ghostly Roman soldier has been seen crossing the road close to Northam Bridge. Another haunting took place in Butts Road, Sholing, where a man with a bicycle asked a passer-by for directions before disappearing before the startled man's eyes. The Anchor Inn in Redbridge is one of the oldest pubs in the area, and it has a long and interesting history, especially when you discover that some of the crew of the Titanic stayed there overnight before embarking on their last ill-fated voyage. People working at the pub have experienced strange sounds and items being moved by an unseen force. The Mayflower theatre is another haunted location, and a man sitting in a wicker chair has been seen backstage at this popular venue. Workers at the Solent Sky Museum have also experience unexplainable phenomena, such as shadowy figures seen lurking between the plane exhibits, as well as the sound of running footsteps when there is nobody there.

We leave Southampton on a lighter note, with the story of a suspected haunting that turned out to be anything but. The story concerns a resident of Millbrook, a Mr Alf Mansbridge who had been spooked by a disembodied voice that kept saying, "I won't take the lift down." This happened at 1:55 am for about 15 minutes every day. Alf, who had been driven to his wits end by this occurrence, actually recorded the voice to prove to his friends and neighbours that he was not losing his marbles. However, after investigation by the local environmental health department, the source of the disembodied voice was eventually traced to a £1.99 child's Spiderman watch that one of Mr Mansbridge's relatives had left at his house!

Swanwick

The Swanwick Train Station Ghost

One night a young man was waiting for the last train home after visiting his girlfriend when he had a strange encounter late one cold Sunday evening. Swanwick station is a small and quite remote station, and on this particular occasion, the young man arrived at around 11 pm, and he was surprised to find another person waiting on the platform, as it was rare for anyone else to be there at that time of night. The other person standing on the platform was a middle-aged woman of around 40 to 50 years old. She was a short plump woman who seemed to be in a distressed state and she asked the young man if there was a train to Portsmouth due, as she needed to get there urgently. Despite the young man's assurances that he was waiting for the same train, and that it would be along in a few minutes, the woman kept asking him the same question, and saying that she "must get back to Portsmouth." When the train did eventually arrived, the woman remained where she was, and despite the young man insisting that this was the last train, the woman became more distressed and refused to move, insisting that she couldn't go back. The young man's offer to help her talk through her problems so long as she boarded the train, seemed to fall on deaf ears, so he had no choice but to leave her behind on the platform. Feeling guilty that he did not do enough to help the woman, upon reaching his destination at Cosham station, the young man decided to call the police at Park Gate police station to inform them that there was a distressed woman on her own at Swanwick train station.

The man thought nothing more of the incident until he arrived home the following evening from work, where his mother drew his attention to the local newspaper, which told the story of a woman who had been killed near to Swanwick station on the preceding Saturday night. The eerie thing was that the description of the deceased matched exactly the woman who the young man encountered on the Sunday night at that very station. Thinking that the reporter must have got their dates mixed up, the man telephoned the newspaper and the police, only to be told that the incident had indeed taken place on Saturday night. It turned out that the woman had been a patient at the local Coldeast mental hospital, and she had been let out to go to Portsmouth. Upon her return, she missed Swanwick station, and she had detrained at the next station (Bursledon). Unfamiliar with the area as she was, the woman decided to trace her way back to Swanwick station by walking along the railway tracks, which unfortunately resulted in her death when the next train came along. Needless to say, when the young man learned that he had possibly encountered the ghost of the recently deceased woman, he decided to get the bus from then on.

Swanwick station. Just make sure that the person you are talking to on the station platform isn't a ghost!

Photo: Basher Eyre

Totton and Eling

<u>Testwood House, Totton</u>

A former royal hunting lodge, Testwood House is situated on the outskirts of Totton, and it is said to be home to a number of ghosts, as well as having a long and chequered history. Local folklore has it that a murder took place in the house more than 200 years ago, although details of the story have changed through years. There are many different versions including the murder of a cook by a manservant or coachman, whilst other versions tell of the death of a butler who was killed during a fight with a coachman over the love of a woman. Whichever version is correct is it their ghosts that now haunt this old building, or are there other spooks lost among the ancient rooms and corridors?

There is no denying that Testwood House has a long and interesting history, and some parts date back to the 15th century, and the Tudor kings Henry VII, Henry VIII and Edward VI all used the house as a base when on hunting expeditions in the New Forest.

Ghostly occurrences have been reported for more than a century, and a Victorian ghost hunter, Stephen Darby, documented cases where a ghostly dog was seen in the driveway. On other occasions, the sounds of unseen horse's hooves and coach wheels chewing up the gravel as if approaching the house in haste, were also heard, and all of this at the turn of the 20th century.

More recent incidents include staff experiencing unease and a strange and rather unpleasant atmosphere in certain parts of the stairs and corridor on the top floor. These stairs and corridors lead to an old attic room, where some people have witnessed the apparition of a female figure during the 1950's. On another occasion, when the property was owned by a company called Williams and Humbert, their caretaker told of an incident where is dog refused to ascend a particular flight of stairs. When the caretaker forced the issue, the dog turned on him and bit him. The caretaker also experienced the sound of heavy footsteps as though somebody was walking on bare floorboards, despite the fact that thick carpets had been laid, and on investigation, he discovered that he was indeed the only person in the locked and empty building.

Eling Tide Mill

There has been a tide mill in Ealing for centuries, and one was even mentioned in the Doomsday Book of 1086, although there is no evidence to say that the mill currently on the site is in fact the same one. However, the mill is one of only two working tide mills in Great Britain, and many people have seen or experienced things that they are at a loss to explain. Many people passing by the mill have mentioned seeing the figure of a man at the window, and some people have reported seeing a ghostly miller at work in the sack loft. Other people have also experienced strange sounds, and one worker explained how as a 15 year old lad, he experienced some strange occurrences whilst working as a millers assistant in 1981. The disembodied sounds of footsteps coming from the area that contains the grain hopper, and the sound of laughter was bad enough, however, the most unsettling experience took place when he turned around to see where the laughter was coming from, only to see a dark shadowy figure walk through the gable end wall.

In 2008, a local paranormal investigation group set up sound recording equipment in certain parts of the mill, and upon examining the recordings, the voice of a young girl can be distinctly heard.

Eling Hill

Another location in the village that is said to be haunted is Ealing Hill, especially the area close to the cemetery that belongs to the church of Saint Mary the Virgin. A number of people have reported seeing a dark shadowy figure glide across the road in front of them when driving down that particular stretch of road. The figure seems to glide across the road as though it has no legs, and it is often observed in the early hours of the morning.

Upham

The Brushmakers Arms

Upham is a small village a few miles south of Winchester, and it used to be famous for being a Mecca for travelling brush makers, thanks in no small part to the quality of the hazel sticks that could be cut from the hedges that lined the lanes and tracks of the Hampshire countryside.

The village has three public houses the most famous of which, is the Brushmakers Arms, which was the inn of choice for the many a weary travelling brush maker.

The spirit that is said to haunt this particular hostelry is said to be the spirit of one of these travelling brush makers, a man named Mr. Chickett, who was a regular at the inn, and he became renowned for two things. The first was the quality of the brushes he produced, and the second was that he was very careful with his money, bordering on miserly so the legend has it. Here was a man who could charge high prices for top quality craftsmanship, and he was never short of a few bob. However, he was extremely protective of his money, going to such lengths as sleeping with his money secreted underneath his pillow.

However, unfortunately for Mr. Chicket, it seems as though this stash of cash was just too tempting for one local ne'er do well who accosted him one night whilst he slept, resulting in Mr. Chicket losing both is money and his life. The crime was never solved, and so the perpetrator remained free, however, Mr. Chicket's restless spirit has been seen and heard on many occasions through the centuries. Shadowy figures have been seen roaming in the rooms where he spent his last night, and dogs have been reluctant to enter the room, and the sound of clinking coins have been heard as though the ghostly Mr. Chicket is still counting his money.

The Brushmakers Arms, Upham

Vernham Dean

The hamlet of Vernham Dean is tucked away in the north corner of Hampshire, and it lies just south of the county's borders with neighbouring Wiltshire and Berkshire. Despite its relatively small size the village did not escape the curse of the Black Death, a disease that ravaged large parts of the country during the 17th century. This was due in no small part to the vast numbers of people who fled the major population centres for the countryside, in order to escape from the pestilence. Unfortunately, however, all they achieved was to spread the disease to these rural communities, and so it was that in 1665 the plague arrived in Vernham Dean. There are no records to state how many of the villages inhabitants succumbed to the illness, but there is a story of how the emergency was handled by the resident pastor.

In order to save the village and prevent the spread of the disease, the village pastor arranged for those affected by the plague to leave the village and head for isolation at nearby Conholt Hill. In return for this, the pastor stated that he would head off to nearby Andover and return with provisions and medicine for the afflicted, as well as promising to bury the deceased and tend to the sick and dying. Unfortunately, the rector never returned to Conholt Hill, and there are two explanations in popular folklore as to why not. One version states that the rector himself was struck down with the plague and never made it to Andover, but the more cynical view was that he reneged on his promise to return in order to save his own life.

Too scared to move in case of divine retribution, and with no help forthcoming, the disease addled villagers perished in isolation and torment. However, it is not the ghosts of these miserable wretches that haunt Vernham Dean, but the spirit of the rector who has been spotted down through the years. Witnesses have often exclaimed that they have seen a small and frail man trudging up the hill, almost bent double as if weighed down by some burden. One can only surmise whether it is the guilt of his cowardice that he carries around with him, or whether it is the provisions that he promised the sufferers in their hour of need.

The Village of Vernham Dean

Warblington

Warblington Parsonage

The ancient village of Warblington has been all but swallowed up by the conurbation we now call Havant Borough. However, the area is home to two very different hauntings. We will come to the ruins of Warblington Castle in a moment, but we shall start this tour at nearby Warblington Parsonage. The original parsonage has long been demolished and it has since been replaced by a building now known as "The Old Rectory". However, the old building was home to a haunting so well known locally, that it deserves its own piece here.

The year was 1695, and the owner of the Parsonage, the Reverend Richard Brereton was desperately trying to find a new tenant for the property, so much so that he was even offering a discount of £10 on the cost of a yearly let. However, such was the reputation of the building within the local community, none of the villagers were tempted to take up the reverend's generous offer. This was due to the fact that most of the villagers remembered how the previous tenants had fled from the building in terror. It transpired that the house was haunted by an evil former parson who fathered a number of illegitimate children by his maid, who he then murdered in cold blood. Ever since then the spot has been haunted by the apparition of a whistling parson.

Warblington Castle Ruins

Warblington Castle was more of a fortified manor house than a proper defensive castle, and it was built for the Countess of Salisbury, Margaret Pole, in the fifteenth century. Unfortunately, the Countess was never fated to live out her life in this splendid building, as she made the mistake of crossing the then monarch Henry VIII over the reformation and the subsequent dissolution of the monasteries.

Instead, she would end her days in the Tower of London, sentenced to death, her final moments on Earth were spent being chased around the scaffold as she refused to kneel for the executioner to do his job. Eventually, she succumbed and her execution was not a pretty sight, with the irate and incompetent executioner finally hacking her head off in a less than swift manner.

As for the house, it passed into a number of hands through the following decades, before eventually being destroyed by Parliamentarian forces during the English Civil War. Now all that remains is one solitary turret, a gate arch and the drawbridge support in the moat, and with the building now on private land, it is not accessible to the public.

When it comes to hauntings, it is the ghost of the unfortunate Margaret Pole who is said to haunt the area. Her apparition is said to be headless, and dressed in a white burial shroud. She has been seen a number of times late at night, but there are also a number of tales about other apparitions in the locale. One is said to be the ghost of a smuggler who was killed in a struggle, and so infamous was the area that it became known as Spook Lane.

Waterlooville

Hulbert Road Apparition

In the Hulbert Road area of the town, a number of people have reported seeing a young woman apparently hitchhiking. On some occasion's people who have stopped to give her a lift on a wet and rainy night, have been left unsettled by the fact that upon reaching the destination the girl had simply vanished, leaving only a wet imprint on the seat.

A more disturbing incident took place in 1976 when a couple who were driving along Hulbert Road on a foggy night were lucky not to have sustained injuries in a road accident. The woman who was driving the car was forced to slam on the brakes after her husband shouted at her to avoid a girl who had suddenly appeared in front of their vehicle. Despite her best efforts to stop the vehicle in time, the pair braced themselves for the inevitable impact, however, there was no sound of a collision, and on closer inspection, there was no sign of any damage to the car, nor was there any sign of the girl, who seemed to have vanished as quickly as she appeared.

The next day, the husband mentioned the incident to work colleagues, who told him that other people had had a similar experience in the same location. The story goes that the apparition is of a young girl who was killed on that stretch of road whilst hitchhiking her way back to Leigh Park.

The Old Drover of Ferndale

Not far from Hulbert Road is Ferndale, a pleasant tree lined avenue in one of the more affluent areas of the town. Yet, even this quiet neighbourhood is home to an unusual haunting, one that appeared at the home of a couple for more than two decades. A couple living in Ferndale (who wished to remain anonymous) witnessed an apparition of an old drover who appeared in their garden on numerous occasions throughout the years.

The first sighting happened in the mid-1970s, when on a lovely warm and sunny morning in May, the lady of the house was vacuuming the living room with the patio doors open, when she experienced a strange feeling of being watched. When she looked into the back garden she saw the figure of a man standing right where the old drovers track used to be located. The figure was dressed in what appeared to be an old fashioned smock and britches, and on his head he was wearing an old and crumpled hat, not too dissimilar to an Australian bushwacker's hat. Thinking that there was a prowler in her garden, the woman was about to call out, but to her surprise, the man vanished in front of her eyes. Despite realising that she had just witnessed the sudden appearance and disappearance of a ghost, the woman explained that she felt no evil, nor was she frightened.

Determined to find out more about who the apparition could be, the woman enquired with the local butcher's deliveryman the next time he called at the house, although she made a point to not mention what she had seen. In fact, she made a point of asking him whether anything tragic or out of the ordinary had happened in the area, only to be told that about a hundred years previously, an old drover committed suicide. The story goes that the man used to regularly drive his cattle along the track from Hambledon to the market in Havant, and one day he disappeared, leaving his cattle to roam free in the local area. When some of the locals went looking for him, they discovered his body swinging from its neck from the branch of an old oak tree.

The woman has speculated that perhaps the spirit of the old drover had been disturbed when a number of old oak trees were felled when the estate was built. The couple and their children have witnessed further manifestations of the old drover either as an apparition or as a sense of sadness, and there is usually a lingering smell of old rough pipe tobacco long after he has disappeared.

Hopfield House

If the ghost in the previous incident was seemingly benign, the one that supposedly haunts Hopfield House is far more malevolent. Hopfield House is a gothic looking building that looks out of place among the more modern and contemporary houses and apartment blocks that have sprung up around it through the years. In fact, from the outside it wouldn't look out of place in one of those old horror movies starring Vincent Price and Peter Cushing.

The house was built by an Edward Fawkes, and the sprawling mansion was constructed with the sole purpose of housing the aforementioned mister Fawkes and his descendents, and only his descendents as it turned out. Problems started when Edward Fawkes' grandchildren broke that tradition by moving to Southsea, and renting the property out to a retired couple on a three year lease. Despite a fairly comfortable first few weeks in their new home, the couple started to feel as though they were not welcome there, culminating in a sighting of an angry Edward Fawkes. The apparition went on to threaten the couple with violence and misfortune should they remain in the property. Despite the threats, the couple put up with the regular appearances of Mr. Fawkes and his malevolent presence before finally calling it a day and moving out for the sake of their sanity. The remainder of the lease was taken over by a middle-aged widow and her daughter who was in her twenties at the time. No one knows whether the angry Edward Fawkes made his presence known to the two new tenants, but misfortune was to befall the woman not long after moving in. Despite being of good health, the widow was found dead in her bed one morning.

By now, the owners of the house were becoming slightly concerned that their ancestor was not being entirely welcoming to the new occupiers of the house. In order to remove the possibility that they could very well be held to account for the problems supposedly affecting the house, the Fawkes decided to wash their hands of the property altogether and put the mansion up for sale.

So it was that the ownership of Hopfield passed into the hands of a man known as Captain Norman Earnest Playfair and his wife Mabel in the early days of 1913. Upon completing the purchase and moving in, the Playfair's renamed the house from 'Hopfield' to 'The Grange', a move that was sure to enrage the late Edward Fawkes even further, and it wasn't long before things started to go wrong for Captain Playfair.

In the first year of ownership of Hopfield House, the previously active and happy Captain Playfair started to show signs of depression and mental instability. There is nothing on record that the captain experienced the wrath of the spirit of Edward Fawkes, but eventually, Captain Playfair would meet a grisly end. There are two versions related to the death of Captain Playfair, with the first one stating that he was killed by being stabbed in the back in a murder that was never sold. The second version is that the heavily depressed Captain took his own life by walking into the hall and stabbing himself in the chest with an ornamental double edged dagger. Either way, this incident along with all the others garnered Hopfield House a reputation as a property that was cursed, and it remained empty for a number of years, with it falling into disrepair in the meantime. The house became infamous locally, with local residents dubbing it as 'the haunted grange' and for that reason it was not until the late 1920s that the house would find a new owner, and it became the property of a Mr. Nowell. However, friends and family of Mr. Nowell desperately tried to convince him to avoid buying the property because of its reputation, and also because of the palpable feeling of evil that seemed to emanate from the house.

Despite the warnings the purchase went ahead, and Mr. Nowell immediately set about restoring the property to its former glory, renovating and expanding the house in order to give it a much more friendly appearance. However, the house seemed to resist any attempts to lighten the atmosphere, and more misery and misfortune would now strike Mr. Nowell and his family, resulting in the suicide of his son, the death of his wife, and then he too would die suddenly in his dressing room, leaving only his daughter Evelyn as the sole survivor. Needless to say, she did not stay in the house for too long, and again the property fell into disrepair. Eventually the house was put into use once more, firstly by the Royal Marine orphanage, before eventually being converted into a number of apartments, which is its current configuration. It seems as though the ghost of Edward Fawkes has been less active in recent years, although some locals maintain that the house still has an evil and foreboding presence about it even now.

Hopfield House, Waterlooville

Winchester

Winchester is an ancient city, and it was once the capital city of Saxon England, and it is home to a number of local legends, which include links to the mystical King Arthur and his knights of the round table. The ancient Normans, Saxons, Romans and Druids have all called the city home through the centuries, and it should come as no surprise that the city has more than its fair share of ghostly goings-on.

Former Hampshire Chronicle Headquarters, High Street

The Hampshire Chronicle is the oldest continuously published newspaper in the county, and it has been in print since the 18th century. It should come as no surprise that its former headquarters was reputedly haunted by two ghosts.

The first is heard more than seen, and is said to be the spirit of a woman, a spirit that likes to make its presence known with the sound of chains rattling.

The other ghost was witnessed by the then sub editor Lesley Park, whilst she was working late one night, here is her story:

"It was 6.30pm and I was getting ready to go home," said Lesley. "I was making my way towards the advertising offices when I saw what I took to be a man standing at the table outside the file room. He appeared to be studying a pile of newspapers. As I watched, the figure turned as if to walk into the file room, which was locked. But when I got to the corridor leading to the file room, it had vanished. Funnily enough, I didn't feel any fear, but if I'd been in the building on my own, it would have been different."

The caretaker at the time was not surprised about Lesley Park's experience, having been in the premises late at night and often on his own, he described the offices as having a spooky feel to them.

The Hampshire Chronicle no longer resides in the building, as they moved to newer premises in 2001, and the building was eventually converted in to flats.

Winchester Cathedral

There are two hauntings that are connected with Winchester Cathedral, the most well-known being the limping monk of Cathedral Close. This apparition has been reported to be seen in and around the area dressed in a brown cloak, and despite having a noticeable limp; this is one apparition that seems to move around quite swiftly.

The second unexplained event concerns a photograph of the inside of the cathedral, and the appearance in the photo of thirteen ghostly figures kneeling as if in prayer at the altar. Taken by a tourist back in 1957, the photograph remains unexplained, and there has been no reasonable or rational explanation as to why these figures appear in the picture.

The Quarry Road Hauntings

A private house in Quarry Road (the number which I have withheld to protect the current occupiers) has reportedly been haunted by as many as three separate ghosts. The most sinister of these apparitions is apparently the ghost of a tall man dressed in a long black coat with brass buttons that seems to possess great strength, and on one occasion a woman and her daughter encountered this ghost on their stairs. Unfortunately, the little girl fell down a flight of 15 steps and broke her leg, and both the girl and her mother were adamant that the ghost had pushed the girl down the stairs on purpose. Other ghosts seen in the property include a nun and a lady in white. There have been many other reported incidents including curtains being drawn by an unseen hand and strange smells. Things got so bad that two exorcisms were carried out during the 1970's to little success.

The Haunted Pubs of Winchester

The Eclipse Inn

Dating back to 1540, the Eclipse Inn has had many uses down through the years, and before it became an Inn it was used as a private house, a rectory and an ale house. Being such an old and well used location, it should come as no surprise that the Eclipse Inn is reputedly haunted by a lady in grey. The Grey Lady is said to haunt the upper corridors of the establishment, and legend has it that it is the spirit of Dame Alice Lisle of Moyles Court.

Lady Lisle was sentenced to death and subsequently executed on 2nd September 1685 for the charge of aiding and abetting traitors connected to the failed Monmouth Rebellion. It was the infamous Judge Jeffrey's who sentenced her to death, and the method of execution was for her to be burnt at the stake. However, after making a personal plea to King James II for clemency, her sentence was changed to a beheading, a far more humane way to be executed at the time. Lady Lisle spent her final night in a room at the top of the building that is now the Eclipse Inn, and it is said that her restless spirit walks the corridor to the room where she spent her final hours on Earth.

The Hyde Tavern

One of the oldest and smallest public houses in Winchester, the Hyde Tavern has at least one ghost and possibly two. People who have stayed overnight in the Inn have reported that they have been the target of a ghost who seems to have a penchant for tugging bedclothes off the bed during the night. The other supernatural occurrence concerns the placing of a cold and clammy hand on to the shoulders of patrons who are drinking in the bar. No one knows whether these two occurrences are connected or caused by separate entities, however, there is a story connected to the Inn that concerns a poor old lady who was turned away after asking for shelter and sustenance, who later died from cold and hunger, and it is her ghost that haunts the Hyde Tavern.

The Jolly Farmer

The Jolly Farmer pub is a pub that can trace its origins back to the 1800s, and it is home to a spook that is known by the name of 'Drunk Henry'. According to folklore, Henry was a well known petty criminal who was eventually arrested, tried, convicted and hanged nearby. Now his spirit is said to haunt the confines of the pub where he spent a lot of his spare time (and the proceeds of his ill-gotten gains). His spirit is a mischievous one who likes to grab drinkers around the shoulders, as well as messing around with the beer pumps behind the bar.

Isle of Wight

The Isle of Wight is usually a place of spectacular countryside, golden beaches and as one of the most popular holiday destinations in the UK. However, it is a place steeped in history and mystery, and it has gained a reputation for being one of the most haunted islands in the world.

Nicknamed 'Ghost Island' the Isle of Wight is home to a plethora of hauntings and spooky goings on, and these include grey ladies, ghostly monks and poltergeist activity. So haunted is the island, that the stars of televisions, Most Haunted team, Yvette Fielding, Derek Accorah et al filmed two episodes there during 2005.

Thanks to the island's uniquely historical past, one full of smugglers, murderers and ancient legends, there are no shortage of great and spine tingling ghost stories to be found here.

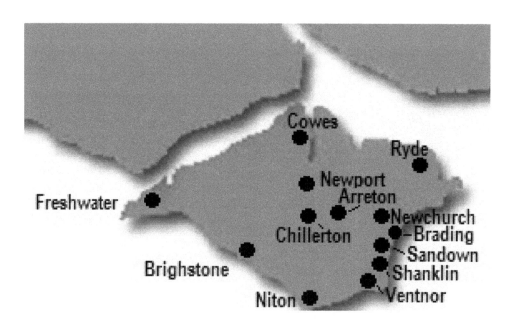

Arreton

Arreton Manor
<u>Arreton Manor</u>

The historic Arreton Manor is one of the most stunning houses on the Isle of Wight, and this Jacobean Manor dates back as far as the year 872. The lanes around the village are palatial, quiet and tranquil, loved by both residents and tourists alike, however, the house holds a dark secret.

In Elizabethan times the house was owned by the wealthy Leigh family, and when the father, Barnaby Leigh fell ill, his son John, hastened the old man's demise in order to inherit his wealth. John dispatched his father by smothering him with a pillow, but his grisly deed was witnessed by his younger sister Annabelle. Panicking, John chased the upset Annabelle upstairs to her room, where he caught her and pushed her from the window to her death. Now it is said that the room where Annabelle spent her last moments alive is always cold, even on the warmest days of the year.

The ghost of the poor unfortunate Annabelle is often seen and heard in and around the house. On occasions, the figure of a small girl dressed in a light blue dress and white slippers has been seen walking through various parts of the house and its grounds on warm summer evenings. On other occasions, people have heard ghostly cries of "Mamma, Mamma..." but for the most part this is a ghost that just seems to be quietly visiting the house that she loved.

It seems as though the ghost of Annabelle is not alone at Arreton Manor, as there have been reports of many other unexplained sightings over the years, which include phantom monks, and several women in various period dress. Visitors have often commented on the fact that they have experienced a strong sense of foreboding when approaching the house, and many have refused to enter. Other people have witnessed monks appearing to glide through the interior walls of the house, as well as the sounds of monks chanting and children crying.

The Hare and Hounds Pub

Three centuries ago, a local woodcutter killed his own grandson in order to get his hands on the boy's inheritance. The story has it that after a number of arguments over the money, the woodcutter by the name of Michael Morey took an axe and murdered the boy in cold blood. In order to cover up his grisly deed, Morey then set fire to the cottage where the incident took place, however, the fire was unsuccessful, and the boys remains were discovered and Morey was subsequently put on trial for murder, found guilty and hanged for his crime. As was the custom at the time, Morey's body was hung from a gibbet which was situated across the road from the pub. Eventually, the corpse became foul smelling and repulsive to look at, and it was taken down and buried in an unmarked grave close by. Now it is said that the ghost of Morey returns to visit the area around the pub, often appearing with rotten skin, ragged clothing and carrying a large axe.

ARRETON MANOR, Isle of Wight

Brading

Brading Waxworks Museum

On the eastern side of the island is the small town of Brading, a coastal town that has a long history and plenty of ghosts. One of the more famous haunted locations in the area could be found at the Brading Waxworks Museum (also known as the Brading Experience and the Osbourne-Smith Wax Museum), a location that has since been demolished. However, during its heyday, the building was a popular local tourist attraction, and before that a well-frequented public house, with the building having been situated on the site since 1499. For most of that time, the building has been home to a number of ghosts, the most famous being the spirit of one Louis de Rochefort.

The story behind the haunting goes back a few hundred years to a time when Brading was a bustling and busy seaport. Back then, the building was an inn known as The Crown, which had a less than squeaky-clean reputation, and it was a venue that was often home to some of the most despicable thieves, vagabonds, gamblers and prostitutes in area.

No one seems to know why a wealthy and well dressed Frenchman such as Louis de Rochefort would find himself in Brading, let alone why he should visit The Crown Inn. However, visit he did, and his wealthy appearance soon attracted the interest of some of the more unscrupulous patrons at the inn. After consuming a hearty meal and several alcoholic drinks, the aforementioned de Rochefort was shown to one of the upstairs bedrooms, where he could rest and spend the night. Sometime during the night, an assailant entered the room and attacked de Rochefort with a large knife. It was said that de Rochefort's dying screams could be heard throughout the building as his attacker made good his escape. Rumours abounded that before he expired, de Rochefort cursed his attacker with his last dying breath and he also swore that he would haunt the building until such a time that his remains would be returned to his homeland and buried.

Down through the years, there have been many reported sightings and sounds that cannot be explained. These included disturbing and blood curdling screams that echoed through the property during the night, whilst other people would comment on seeing a shadowy, tall and well-dressed figure in one of the bedrooms. There was also said to be the sound of an invisible coach and horses, which could be heard approaching the front of the property.

The hauntings continued into modern times, with at least one resident unable to cope with the disturbing experiences and having to leave the property in a hurry. In addition to which, dogs were often said to react to "something" unseen on the first floor of the building.

In 1964 workmen who were installing a water main unearthed a human skeleton. By this time, the building was owned by Graham Osborne-Smith who had turned the building into a waxworks museum. It was his idea to send the skeleton back to France for burial, however, no descendents of Louis could be located in his home town of Rochefort, and the bones were returned to Brading, where Osborne-Smith exhibited them in the museum, and where the museum staff nicknamed the unfortunate skeleton, "Lonely Louis".

Brighstone

The Capricorn Club

The phantom of a military officer, which was often seen standing around the bar, is said to be a man who was tragically killed on the site during a German bombing raid during World War II.

The Three Bishops Inn

Once named The New Inn; this popular watering hole was renamed sometime during 1973 after three local vicars had been appointed bishops in other parts of the country. One rector who lived and worked in the area was a Samuel Wilberforce, who just happened to be the son of William Wilberforce, MP, and Samuel would become Bishop of Oxford. Bishop Thomas Ken wrote the immortal hymn, "Awake my soul and the sun", during his stopover here between 1667 and 1669. He would later become the Bishop of Bath and Wells, and the third was George Moberley, who would later be appointed as the Bishop of Salisbury. Hauntings are provided by the spirit of one of the former proprietors, a certain Maggie Hawker, who was in residence sometime during the 1950's. She often appears whilst muttering to herself, and she has a habit of unlocking all of the doors before she disappears again.

Chillerton

<u>Billingham Manor</u>

The aptly named village of Chillerton is situated between Newport and Chale and is home to Billingham Manor, one of the most haunted manor houses on the island. The manor house is over 250 years old, and local legends tell of it being the hideaway of the deposed Charles I after he managed to escape from his confinement at nearby Carisbrooke Castle. In order to escape detection, Charles was said to have been concealed in a very narrow hideaway that was hidden behind a removable wall panel in the drawing room. It was said that so narrow and cramped was this hideaway that Charles opted to leave and return to his dungeon at Carisbrooke Castle, in the forlorn hope that a ship might take him to France. Whether or not there was any truth in the story, there is no disputing the fact that a very confined space, no bigger than a coffin, was discovered behind a secret panel in the drawing room by one of the inhabitants Sir Shane and Lady Leslie in 1928. In fact, the pair were often disturbed by some strange and rather unsettling noises during the night, which included the sounds of clanking swords, and the thud of heavy footsteps on the stairs. In addition to which, a maid in their employ reported seeing a figure walk through a wall into another room. Nevertheless, as chilling as these experiences were, the worst and most unsettling was yet to come.

In the early hours of one particular morning, with the ghostly noises becoming so loud as to wake up everyone who was present in the house, Sir Shane and Lady Leslie as well as several others, made their way to the drawing room, where the noises were at their loudest. Upon their arrival in the room, everyone noticed a strange faint glow emanating from the gaps around the hidden panel in the wall, the very location where Charles I's hiding place was located. Upon removing the panel the resultant light was so bright as to temporarily blind the entire party, but when their sight eventually returned, they were left with the unsettling sight of Charles I's disembodied head staring out at them from the recess!

There is a strange twist to this story, when Sir Shane Leslie was conducting research into the manor house, he discovered the diaries of a former owner. In the diaries, Sir Shane uncovered the fact that this former owner had also experienced this particular phenomenon on two separate occasions. The diarist also recorded the fact that on both occasions that the apparition was witnessed, there had been an execution on the island, and to Sir Shane's amazement, an execution had also taken place in Newport on the day of his sighting of the apparition. There have been no further recorded sightings since capital punishment was abolished in the UK in 1965.

One of Billingham Manor's most famous non-ethereal residents was the writer J. B. Priestley who stayed at the house when writing some of his books. He always insisted that he never saw anything out of the ordinary, although he never put on record whether he had indeed heard anything. In fact at the time of his frequent stays, strange noises were often heard in various locations throughout the house, as well as several people, which included the authors own son, reporting the sighting of a strange smiling lady.

Other residents of the house have also claimed to have encountered this strange smirking woman, as well as the figure of a hooded monk, and there has been other strange unexplained phenomena reported down through the years as well. This includes the sudden scent of Madonna Lillies, as well as various noises such as the sound of heavy footsteps and furniture being moved around. These occurrences have been linked to the smiling lady, and it is thought that she is the spirit of a woman who was involved in a love triangle. Local legend has it that a Miss Leigh married a member of the Worsley family who were resident at the house during the early 1700s. However, Miss Leigh also became romantically involved with a French nobleman, and one day their tryst was discovered by her husband. A duel to the death ensued, and it was the French nobleman who received a fatal wound. After his victory, Miss Leigh was forbidden by her husband from leaving Billingham Manor ever again, and that is where she remained for the rest of her life. Now it is said that the poor woman's spirit walks the halls and rooms of the old house, the scent of her favourite Madonna lilies accompanying her.

Billingham Manor

Cowes

Northwood House and Park

The stunningly beautiful Northwood House and the surrounding parkland that it is situated in make it an ideal venue for weddings and other celebrations and events. Yet, there are one or two visitors who are not there by invitation, and if you are lucky enough to be visiting at the right time, you may be able to hear the sound of children playing in the park, even though there are no children there. Many people have reported hearing the excited screams of playing children at dusk, even though there have been no sign of children in the immediate vicinity. It is said that the noises are from a group of boys who died from Spanish Flu in 1918, and the playful sounds are them in happier days climbing trees and playing.

Another ghost that has been reported appears in the house itself. The apparition of a grinning pirate has been seen in the vast cellars of Northwood House, and he is always wearing a striped top, black boots, a single earring and a knotted scarf around his neck. He may also be responsible for the sound of large wooden barrels being rolled around in the basement.

Shooters Hill

There are two haunted locations in the Shooters Hill area of Cowes, including the haunting of the Jolliffe's former shoe shop building. The building is an attractive Art Deco structure which is now an art gallery and coffee house. The apparition in question is said to be one of the original owners of the shop who appears in the upper parts of the building, and it takes the form of an elderly man who spooks visitors by disappearing before their eyes.

A number of other dwellings in Shooters Hill are also subject to some unearthly occurrences, and a girl in Victorian style dress has been seen in a number of various locations, and it is alleged that she is responsible for moving objects from one property to another.

East Cowes Airfield

The now disused airfield was allegedly haunted by a spectre so terrifying that it severely shocked those who were unfortunate enough to witness it. The airfield had been in the front line during World War II, but it would eventually be closed, and it is now home to a number of companies involved in the aerospace industry. The hauntings in question took place many years after the end of the war, but whilst the airfield was still being used, although it would be mostly quiet at night, save for the intermittent movement of planes being readied for flight the following day.

The first sighting of the apparition took place when a group of pilots visited the airfield and both they and the permanent personnel stationed there were drawn to look up at the night sky. What they saw startled them at first, as they could see the silhouette of a parachutist coming into land. As the apparition got closer to the ground, the group's mood changed from startled to terrified, as they saw that the figure was headless! This apparition has been seen before, typically just before his feet hit the ground or after he has landed, then the chute collapses around him and he vanishes.

People who have reported seeing this apparition have often been subject to ridicule, and the story has been dismissed as an urban legend or the product of an overactive imagination. However, those who dismiss this story would do well to take note of another incident involving this spectre, a security guard and his dog. One night, the security guard was doing his rounds as normal, when the dog suddenly looked up into the night sky. Upon witnessing the approaching headless parachutist, the dog howled and went frantic, eventually tearing free of his handler and running off. When the security guard eventually caught up with the dog, the animal was going berserk and sadly had to be put down.

The Anchor Inn

This inn dates back to the first decade of the 18th century and was once named the House of the Three Trumpeters. The inn acquired this name as it was Cowes main coaching inn, and of course the bugle horn was used to signal the arrival or departure of the mail coach. However, by the 1820's the pub had its name changed to the Anchor, and the area used as the stables was integrated into the main pub, taking the imaginatively titled name of the Stable Bar. Now this particular area of the pub is supposedly haunted by the restless sprit of a young man who committed suicide over a failed love affair. Witnesses have described the manifestation as being a young man with fair hair, who is wearing a white shirt and dark trousers.

The Union Inn

This particular inn has been around since the late 1700's and due to its location close to the water it was often popular with smugglers. In fact, at some point in its long history, the pub used to house a light tower, which would be left burning at night in order to help weary fishermen find their way safely back to shore in rough seas. When the tower keeper was offshore, his wife would take over the task of making sure that the light was burning in his absence. Unfortunately, one night she forgot, and many sailors lost their lives, including her husband who drowned. Now it is said that the sorrowful woman can be seen climbing the steps to the long since vanished light tower in order to check if the light is burning.

Freshwater

Golden Hill Fort

Situated not far from the village of Freshwater lies another of the many forts that once made up the Palmerston defences, which in 1859 was instigated by the Royal Commission on the defence of the United Kingdom. This instigated the construction of a number of defensive forts along the south coast, the primary use of which were to repel invaders from the continent (mainly the French), however, by the time the construction had been completed, this threat had largely passed, and these fortifications were never needed, eventually earning the nickname, Palmerston's Follies.

Despite the lack of an invasion, Golden Hill Fort was still used as a barracks, and a number of witnesses have reported strange occurrences that cannot be explained.

As you would expect from such an old and historic venue, there are a number of legends attached to the property, and some of these legends are likely to have been connected in some way to the unusual happenings at the fort. For example, there is the story of a Sergeant Major, who during the First World War was stationed at the fort. So unpopular was he among his troop, that he met an "accidental" end, falling down one of the fort's narrow and steep spiral staircases, fatally breaking his neck in the process. Another legend concerns the imprisonment and execution of a treacherous sailor, who was caught trying to sell military secrets to an enemy agent and subsequently hanged for his crime. Now it is said that the spirits of these two men often revisit the place of their demise. Some of the unexplained occurrences at the fort include the smell of pipe tobacco smoke, hot and cold spots, phantom footsteps, and locked doors seemingly opening of their own volition. More disconcertingly, the apparition of a sailor has been spotted standing in one of the doorways with his arms folded across his chest.

Needles Old Battery

A short distance from Freshwater is Alum Bay, home to the Needles Old Battery, a fortification built high up on the cliffs overlooking the Needles. Constructed during the height of hysteria over a possible invasion attempt by France in the 1860s, the fort is now one of the islands most well-known tourist attractions. It is also said to be haunted by ghostly soldiers who are dressed in World War I uniform. These spectres have been witnessed running along the 60 metre tunnel that leads to the searchlight post above the Needles rocks. The area is also apparently home to a ghostly car, which has been seen, decked in wartime camouflage driving very slowly and in near total darkness down the winding and narrow road that leads to the fort.

Newchurch

Knighton Gorges Manor

Just outside the village of Newchurch is a location that claims to be one of the most haunted locations on the island, Knighton Gorges Manor. Given that the island itself is often said to be the most haunted island in the world, this is not a claim to be taken lightly. The manor house has long gone, but the site still retains an air of mystery, and there have been multiple sightings of an unusual nature in the area where the house once stood.

The manor house was originally built in the 12 century, and was one of the most ornate and architecturally significant buildings on the island, and quite possibly in the entire south of the country at the time. However, the house soon became synonymous with tragic events, culminating in the destruction of the house by arson, sometime in 1821. The house was destroyed by its owner, a man by the name of George Maurice, a man who torched his own home prior to his death in order to prevent his daughter from inheriting the property, due to the fact that he disagreed with her choice of husband (a clergyman).

Now that the manor house has long since been demolished, all that remains to remind people that it once stood there are the two remaining stone gateposts. These gateposts themselves have been said to be a focal point for ghostly goings-on, with a number of people reporting the sighting of animal figures or gargoyles sitting on top of the posts. If such additions where ever added to these posts remains unclear, and if they were, they were obviously removed sometime in the past, as all that remains now is plain stone.

In addition to ghostly gargoyles, there have also been a number of sightings of other apparitions in the immediate vicinity. These include the supposed sighting of the ghost of Sir Tristram Dillington, who was a Member of Parliament for Newport. He was reported to have committed suicide after failing to recover from the death of his wife, and it was his valet who discovered his body. In order to avoid an inquest into his death, and to stop the house being forfeited, the valet took the cadaver and placed it upon his horse (named Thunderbolt), and drove it into the lake. Now, locals and ghost hunters alike say that they have been witness to the ghost of Sir Tristram riding his horse into the lake, a scene that is said to reoccur on 7th July, the date of his death in 1721.

One of the main hauntings connected to Knighton Gorges is concerns the reappearance of the entire house, with a party seemingly in full swing! This event is said to happen every New Years Eve, and it has such a reputation that crowds of people often gather in the area in order to witness the event.

Other unexplained events that have been reported include the sound of a coach and horses galloping up the drive, the sighting of a woman in a purple dress, believed to be the daughter of one of the owners, as well as unexplained lights and orbs visible in the night sky.

All that remains of Knighton Gorges Manor is a couple of gateposts

Photo: Naturenet

Newport

The Ghost Train

The Newport to Cowes railway line was the very first railway line to open on the island in 1862, linking two of the major population centres of the island together, and also allowing for easier access to ferries to Southampton. Eventually, the line became a victim to the Beeching cuts, and the line was closed to all traffic in 1966. However, it seems as though one train does not want to go quietly. People who live in the area around Gordon Road, where the line used to run along the bottom of their gardens, have claimed to have heard and seen a steam train with three carriages, hurtling along the now long removed track.

The Castle Inn

The oldest pub in Newport, the Castle Inn is said to be haunted by the ghost of a long-dead stable lad who it is claimed was a victim of what is known as Jeddard Justice. Jeddard (or Jethart as it is sometime called) is an ancient form of justice where a person was hanged before their trial. However, the official line on his death was that he committed suicide due to the emotional turmoil from a failed love affair. It was the result of a paranormal investigation that brought to light the fact that the victim was in fact killed after being attacked by three men and a woman. It was a medium who allegedly made contact with the unfortunate stable lad's restless spirit, and it was him who mentioned the words Jethart Justice. Apparently, he owed money to the woman, and when it became apparent that he could not repay his debt, the woman had him strung up from one of the high beams in the stables, where he eventually died of asphyxiation.

Nowadays, the spirit is often heard whistling in the early hours of the morning, something that has been heard by a number of different landlords of the pub through the years. Upon investigating, the subsequent check for intruders typically reveals that everything in the pub is peaceful, expect for a number of five pence pieces being strewn about the place. It is thought that the five pence pieces resemble one of the coins that were in circulation at the time of the stable lad's demise in the 18th century, and it seems that he is still trying to pay off his debt.

Carisbrooke Castle

For more than nine centuries Carisbrooke Castle has stood firm against attack, but within its stone walls and Keep, its ghosts roam. In the famous well-house where donkeys work the wooden treadwheel, the face of a long-dead girl, Elizabeth Ruffin, who drowned in the 160ft deep well, has been seen. A mysterious figure in a long cloak, with four dainty lap dogs, walks the castle grounds, while the ghost of a young man wearing brown jerkin and trousers is seen near the moat. Other phantoms include a Victorian lady in grey, a Royal Princess and a presence in the Castle gatehouse.

Whitecroft Hospital

Just outside Newport to the south lies the site of the former Whitecroft Hospital. The hospital was the local lunatic asylum, and it was a large imposing gothic building that was said to house a number of its former patients. Nowadays, the building has been converted into luxury apartments and goes by the name of Gatcombe Manor. Nevertheless, in the days before the hospital was closed, a number of staff reported strange occurrences that could not be fully explained. Situated behind the main hospital building was the nurse's accommodation block, where residents often reported that the doors would open and close of their own accord.

Workmen who were on site during the conversion of the buildings to residential status often reported that their tools would vanish, with many men saying that tools would move in front of their eyes as if moved by some unseen hand. One of the areas that seemed to suffer most from ghostly goings-on was the clock tower, and many workmen refused to work in this location.

Other unexplained phenomena include the sightings of a hazy white figure that moves across the site of the old car park, which was located near to the old laundry building. Apparently, this spook is the ghost of one of the former doctors who worked at the building, and he was often seen peering into one of the empty rooms before disappearing suddenly.

Several people have also laid claim to witnessing the sprinting spook of a young man in his twenties, and another former member of staff has also been seen in one of the old patient wards. This apparition is said to be well dressed in a dark suit with cravat, topped off with an unkempt mop of hair. He has been seen walking quickly along the first floor corridors of the wards, closely followed by one of his former assistants, so it appears that you get two ghosts for the price of one in this location!

The Wheatsheaf Hotel

This historical former coaching inn can trace its history back to the 17th century and is home to a number of apparitions, as well as reported poltergeist activity. The most famous ghost to haunt this venue is the spectre of a former army officer, who apparently died during a duel that took place sometime in the 19th century. The story goes that this deadly duel took place in the early 1800s between two officers, at dawn in the grounds of nearby Carisbrooke Castle. Both men fired, however, only one received a wound. The wounded man was taken to the Wheatsheaf Hotel in order to recover from his injuries. Unfortunately, the officer had been shot through a lung and spinal cord, and despite the best efforts of a local doctor, the man died from his wounds. Now, the ghost of the deceased officer walks the middle floor of the building, dressed in trousers with a stripe and a white open necked shirt. Many people have also stated that his appearance is accompanied by a shrieking sound that is said to be the distraught cry of his young widow.

The hotel is also said to be haunted by the ghost of a young woman, who appears dressed in a servant's attire. She is often seen sitting on the end of a bed on the first floor at night, accompanied by the sounds of chains being dragged across a hard floor.

The Wheatsheaf Hotel, Newport

Niton

St. Catherine's Lighthouse

This lighthouse is officially the most southerly part of the island, and it is also one of the most haunted lighthouses in southern England. This white octagonal lighthouse has a light that can be seen by shipping as far as 26 nautical miles away. This is thanks to having a light that is the third most powerful in all of the lighthouses owned and operated by Trinity House, with a light as bright as 1 million candles.

A lighthouse has been on this site since the fourteenth century, but this particular building has been in constant operation since 1875, apart from during World War II when the light was extinguished in order to prevent enemy bomber crews using it for navigation purposes. The light was only ever switched on during this period when it was known that allied shipping convoys were passing by.

During the war, Niton was also an important location as part of the Chain Home radar network, and was often the target of enemy air attacks. One such attack in 1943 nearly put the light out of action for good, and the damage caused to the reflector can still be seen to this day. Tragedy struck during this raid as a bomb landed on the building that was used as the emergency power boiler room, where the three lighthouse keepers were in at the time. All three were killed instantly, and were buried together in the nearby Niton churchyard.

Maybe it was the spirit of one of these deceased lighthouse keepers that a telephone engineer captured on a photograph that he took in the early 1990's. Having no prior knowledge of the tragic events that took place a half century before, the engineer was leaving the lighthouse late one afternoon after spending a few hours installing a new telephone system. The engineer decided to take a couple of snaps of the imposing building in the early evening gloom. However, it wasn't until he got the film developed a few weeks later that he had the shock of his life, as there in the lantern room, silhouetted against the bright light, stands the lone figure of a man.

The engineer is adamant that when he locked up the lighthouse upon leaving that there were no other people in the building, and the photograph has been scrutinised by experts, who have come to the conclusion that it has not been tampered with in any way.

The Buddle Inn

This inn dates back over 400 years originally as a farm, but it later became a drinking establishment famed for being popular with smugglers, thanks to its location on the south coast of the island.

Visit the inn now, and you will be greeted with a pub that is like a step back in time, with its original flagstone flooring, old oak beams on the ceiling, and its large fireplace. It is one of those places where you can sit and enjoy a drink on a blustery winter evening and believe in tales of smugglers and ghosts.

In fact, you do not have to imagine stories about ghosts, as a number of people have stated that they have witnessed figures, which walk across the bar and through a wall at the far end. On other occasions, people have reported seeing apparitions that appear to be wearing old fashioned clothing, some dressed like smugglers, whilst others are said to be dressed as sailors and customs officers.

Ryde

<u>The Priory Bay Hotel, Seaview</u>

Just outside Ryde is the quaint town of Seaview, and here you will find the Priory Bay Hotel. A medieval priory once stood on this site, and now the hotel is said to be haunted by the ghost of the blue lady who met her untimely death as a young girl and her beloved pet dog.

The following article is taken from the Priory Bay Hotel's own website, and was originally taken from an article by Sheila White: -

The Blue Lady

The Priory belonged to a branch of my grandmother's family, from the Grose-Smith's (on my father's side) in the early 1700s until the last member of the family to live there (my father's cousin Laura Spencer-Edwards) died in the 1920s. The Priory then, alas, passed out of our hands forever.

I have never lived at The Priory but used to visit, with my parents, as a small girl and loved every stick and stone of the place. It had everything an old house ought, tales of secret rooms, secret passages, buried treasure, smugglers and, of course, and the ghost!

She, indeed, was the main attraction at The Priory for me: her portrait, full length and almost life-size, hung in the dining room. It depicted a girl of about fourteen or fifteen years old with a little pointed, heart shaped face, seated in a garden, a small canary fastened to one finger by a narrow satin ribbon and a King Charles Spaniel playing at her feet.

Whether or not my cousin knew her real name, I never found out. I never pressed the matter, sensing somehow that that was how she herself preferred it and being perfectly happy myself always to think of her as The Blue Lady.

As for being afraid of her, that was quite impossible for I adored her and would stand transfixed before her portrait gazing up at the little smiling face feeling a strange affinity with her, longing to know more about her and hoping against hope that one day I might see her.

Cousin Laura said she was usually seen tripping down the main staircase or crossing the hall; at other times she was seen flitting about the gardens and quite often on especially frosty starlit nights, gliding soundlessly along the road and across the fields in the direction of the house where I now live, which was once part of The Priory Estate.

It is now over half a century since I stayed at The Priory and in those days lamps and candles were the order of the day, or rather, the night. Every evening the maids placed rows of silver candlesticks with candle snuffers (chamber-sticks I believe is the right word and they are worth a small fortune today) on a chest in the hall right below a stuffed dog in a glass case by the main staircase!

When bedtime came, I would collect my candlestick and light the candle with trembling fingers, trying desperately not to look up and catch the baleful eye of the dog. But, as I went up the stairs, I always found my gaze directed to him and as the candlestick shaking in my hand caused the flame to flicker, it made the dog look as though he were moving. At this point I would race up the remaining stairs as fast as I could to the safety of my room!

We used to wonder sometimes if this dog could really be the original dog belonging to The Blue Lady: he certainly looked a bit worn in parts, but could he really have survived the centuries – certainly two, but possibly three – and still be in one piece? I have no doubts now.

Now comes the really strange part of the story and this, oddly enough, did not arise until after cousin Laura's death and The

Priory was no longer ours. After her death in 1927, The Priory was sold and a very wealthy and charming American lady whom I will simply call Mrs S bought it. One day, we received an invitation to take tea with her, so my grandmother, my mother and I set off to walk through the fields on a lovely summer day. The door was opened to us by a butler who led us into what had been the dining room – where the portrait of The Blue Lady had hung – but which Mrs S had now turned into her drawing room adding to it extensively and putting in some hideous new eight-sided windows that put my teeth on edge. But she herself was charming.

She welcomed us from her wheelchair, behind which stood her Secretary, and beside which stood her magnificent Great Dane, Shadow. It was during tea that she suddenly leant across the table and said, "Is this place haunted?"

I replied that it was. "Don't tell me by what," she said quickly, "hear my story first."

She then proceeded to tell the following incredible tale: it appears that after settling into The Priory, her servants began to give notice. This was not very alarming in those days as there was still plenty of domestic help available. They were replaced as they left and nothing thought of it, except that they probably found life on the Island too dull after London.

It was when her butler, who had been with her for many years, handed in his notice that she realised that there must be something seriously wrong and instantly sent for him to find out his reasons for wishing to leave.

"Do you find it too quiet over here, too cut-off from your friends and family?" she asked. But it was not that.

"It is the noises, Madam," he told her. "Every night, in the early hours of the morning we hear a child running through the passages crying and sobbing for her dog." He went on to tell her that as they opened their bedroom doors and gone out into the passages, the footsteps had actually passed them and the sobbing had been heart-rending.

"We clearly hear the words, my dog, my dog, what have you done with my dog," he went on, "and it was more than flesh and blood could stand." It was obvious that the place was haunted.

Now Mrs S was an intelligent, level-headed businesswoman and she made up her mind, there and then, to get to the bottom of this story. She made enquiries all around the village and found that it was common knowledge that The Priory was haunted. But most people only spoke of a Grey Lady and were very vague as to what she was supposed to do.

In the end, she suddenly switched her researching to the dog. Did anyone know anything about a dog connected with the place - any dog – anything to do with a dog, if so, please let her know?

Many people remembered that cousin Laura had had an Airedale, but this was dismissed as having nothing to do with the haunting at all and she was nowhere near a solution to the problem until suddenly, Mr C who was head gardener at The Priory and had been gardener's boy there at the age of thirteen, remembered that there had been a stuffed dog in a glass case hanging over the stairs!

This was what she had been waiting for. Instantly Mrs S went into action. The distant cousin who had inherited The Priory was contacted and asked if he had taken the dog.

He remembered it and thought it must have been sold at auction with all the other things not wanted by the family.

There followed an advertisement in the local papers, which

ended in the dog being traced back to an antique shop in Newport. It was then bought back to The Priory and replaced in its old place over the stairs and from that moment all noises ceased.

"So," said Mrs S, "tell me who – or what – haunts this place?" We then told her the story of The Blue Lady who had died when still a child and the stuffed dog, said to be hers, which certainly bore a resemblance to the dog in the portrait.

The Ryde Castle Hotel

This castellated building dates back to Tudor times and the reign of Henry VIII, and it was built as an extra fortification, its main aim being to protect the Spithead and the Solent from French attacks. In addition to this, the building also saw service during the two world wars, as a hospital during World War I, and as a command centre during World War II.

These days it is a popular hotel, but as well as being home to paying guests there are said to be a number of ghosts also staying here. One ghost in particular is fond of playing pranks on guests and staff alike, however, some of the ghosts are said to be the restless spirits of some of the soldiers and sailors who died here during the two world wars. Maybe it was one of these ghosts who caused the near total destruction of the building in March 2012. The roof of the building caught fire one evening, and the conflagration quickly spread to the rest of the building. Despite the best efforts of more than 50 firefighters the building was gutted. There is probably no ghostly explanation for the fire starting and the cause was most likely to be fireworks that were being let off from the roof due to a wedding reception taking place at the time.

Sandown

<u>Sandown Pier</u>

The pier was originally built in the late 1870s but only extended to just over 105 metres due to the fact that the Sandown Pier Company, set up to fund and operate the pier, ran out of money. It wasn't until the 1930s that the pier was extended, and this extension included the construction of a 1,000 seat pavilion, near to the shore, with the original situated at the pierhead, becoming a ballroom.

When the swinging 60s arrived, the pier could boast the largest theatre on the island, a 980 seat venue that would host many of the biggest names in entertainment at the time, including such luminaries as Bob Monkhouse, Cilla Black and Jimmy Tarbuck. However, it was two lesser known entertainers who first spotted the ghost of the theatre. Impressionist Marc Duane and entertainer John Martin noticed a ghostly apparition on stage one evening after their show had finished. Looking towards the stage they saw the figure of a man standing in the centre of the stage who appeared to be just laughing. The man then turned around and left the stage by walking straight through the curtain, leaving it totally undisturbed, which is more than could be said for the two witnesses. The two men also noticed that the area had become icy cold, and that this was not practical joke being played on them by somebody else.

Another incident on the pier took place a number of decades later when in 2011 a man took a photo of the pier, and when he took a look at the picture he noticed the image of an old woman. The man who took the photo was adamant that there was nobody stood there at the time.

Isle of Wight Zoo

Formerly called Sandown Zoo and the Isle of Wight Tiger and Lemur Sanctuary, this zoo is actually built within an old fortification, part of the infamous Palmerston defences. It is this previous use as a fort that connects the current zoo with its ghost. It is claimed that the location is haunted by the ghost of a young soldier who lost his life when the cannon he was test firing malfunctioned and decapitated him (other versions of the story claim that he was in fact cut in half, either way it wasn't a pleasant end). Now it is claimed that his restless spirit haunts the location of the old gun emplacement near the moat.

Shanklin

The Crab Inn, Shanklin

This grade II listed building either got its name from the edible crustacean or from a type of winch that had projecting arms, giving it a crab-like appearance. Either way, this is a pleasant looking building, thatched, and with wood panelling and flagstone flooring. People visiting or staying at the inn have reported a number of unexplained occurrences, these include having their hair pulled whilst sitting at a certain table, the apparition of a lady in white, and sudden drops in temperature even on the hottest days of the year.

The Bourne Hall Country Hotel, Shanklin

One couple who stayed in room 25 of this hotel experienced something rather unusual. Here is the entry that they left on the review website Tripadvisor :-

> Neither of us believed in ghosts before this night. We woke in the morning, and both had a similar dream about a corner of the room where a picture hung. Noticing the picture wasn't up the right way, I turned it around so the fleur de lys were the right way up. Whilst we were both in the room, it changed back - we didn't see it! I asked my partner to put the kettle on, and the switch flipped itself - pretty impossible as it was quite stiff. My partner said he spent the whole second night feeling watched from one corner. As I said, none of us believe in ghosts, well, we didn't!

Ventnor

Ventnor Botanical Gardens

The Ventnor Botanical Gardens is classed as being one of the most haunted locations on the Isle of Wight, and this is partly due to the history of the site as for nearly 100 years it housed the Royal National Hospital. The hospital was one of the most important of its kind in the UK, which was dealing with infectious diseases such as tuberculosis.

The hospital was home to a lot of experimental and pioneering treatments and surgeries in the fight against TB, however, despite these successes, there was no shortage of fatalities from consumption.

The final patient left in the 1964, and a few years later all of the hospital buildings were demolished, and Ventnor Botanical Gardens was born, and with it came the ghost stories.

The hospital buildings were haunted, and now, as they were being torn down, there were a number of reports of strange happenings. The area where the majority of strange events took place was the building that originally housed the operating theatre, which was the final building to be demolished on the whole site. The building itself even seemed to resist all attempts to knock it down, with excavators, tractors and wrecking ball crane all damaged during the demolition.

Workers often had strange experiences in and around the operating theatre building, including two men who were spooked by a figure standing in a doorway as they were preparing to commence demolition with a pair of sledgehammers.

On other occasions, workmen often spotted a ghostly young girl who looked pale, sickly and hollow eyed, who would watch them going about their work. Many of these workers where tough, grizzled me who did not scare easily, nevertheless, there were few of them who would leave before it got dark.

It wasn't just the workmen who were having problems, the locals would often complain about the noise, and not the sound of the demolition work either, but the sounds of groaning and moaning coming from the vacant hospital buildings at during the night!

Other strange occurrences in the area included sudden drops in temperature, strange feelings of unease and dread, as well as the sighting of misty silhouettes, which were often spotted gliding around the ruins of the old buildings.

Eventually, the area was levelled off and a car park built over the top. However, despite there being no trace of the former operating theatre building, unusual things continued to happen.

On one occasion, a man sent by the council to survey the area, was shocked to see the image of two woman dressed in Victorian nurses clothing pass in front of him. On another occasion, an electrician who was working on the site went to make use of the toilet facilities, which were in an area that used to house the former hospitals shop. Whilst letting nature take its course, the man was shocked to see a ghost sitting on top of the cubicle door. The man was so unsettled by this experience that he rushed out of the toilet block, still with his trousers unfastened, jumped into his vehicle and he was never to return.

These days, the botanical gardens are one of the most visited places on the island, but not all visitors are there to just enjoy the palatial surroundings. The Ventnor Botanical Gardens has become a magnet for ghost hunters, mediums and spiritualists alike, and many of them come from hundreds of miles away, just to get a feel of the place.

With the car park in situ, most visitors are blissfully unaware of the fact that the hospital even stood on the site, yet the old operating theatre still seems to exert an eerie presence on the area. Dogs, who are often more susceptible to the paranormal, will often baulk when their owners have tried to lead them across the car park. The car park is also the area where the most accidents seem to take place.

To this day, people often report feelings of being watched, whilst others have reported being touched by unseen hands, whilst there are still reports of people seeing ghostly figures, or smelling the unmistakable scent of ether.

Top and Middle: Ventnor Botanical Gardens in its previous existence as a specialist lung diseases hospital.

Bottom: The modern day car park, which is situated on the site of the old hospital operating theatre, and where many strange events take place today.

Wroxall

<u>Appuldurcombe House</u>

This 18th century country house is now just a shell, but it was once the seat of the Worsley family, and there has been a building on the site dating back to 1100. The shell of the house that is currently owned by English Heritage, and is open to the public, dates back to the early 1700s.

During the two world wars troops were billeted here, but unfortunately, the house received severe damage from a German bombing raid during World War II.

It is claimed that the site and the remains of the house in particular, are among the most haunted on the entire island, and the house was even visited by the Most Haunted team for a series 6 investigation back in 2005.

Hauntings that have been reported include an apparition that is quite often seen running up and down stairs.

The cellars are said to be among the most haunted locations in the house, and many people have reported feelings of unease, dread and of being watched. There have also been reports of fleeting glimpses of figures lurking in the shadows.

Other strange occurrences include the sighting of two boys who were unfortunately killed due to a gunpowder explosion in 1567. Their spirits have been seen in the area of the gate house.

Other witnesses have reported seeing the ghostly image of a grey monk, who walks across the laws carrying a lit lantern on a pole.

Bibliography

Publications

Brodie, A, 1981. *Haunted Hampshire*. 1st ed. UK: J. W. Arrowsmith.
Brandon & Brooke, 2010. *Shadows in the Steam: The Haunted Railways of Britain*. 1st ed. UK: The History Press.
Forman, J, 1989. *The Haunted South*. 1st ed. UK: Jarrold.
Legg, P, 2011. *Haunted Southampton*. 1st ed. UK: The History Press.
Long, R, 1999. *Haunted Inns of Hampshire*. 1st ed. UK: Power Publications.
Underwood, P, 1983. *Ghosts of Hampshire and the Isle of Wight*. 1st ed. UK: Abbey Press.
Underwood, P, 2014. *Where the Ghosts Walk: The Gazetteer of Haunted Britain*. 1st ed. UK: Souvenir Press Ltd.
Westwood & Simpson, J, 2005. *The Penguin Book of Ghosts*. 1st ed. UK: Penguin.

Internet Sites

www.paranormaldatabase.com
www.wikipedia.org
www.sourthernlife.org.uk
www.mysteriousbritain.co.uk
www.dailyecho.co.uk
www.dailymail.co.uk
www.telegraph.co.uk
www.hampshire-history.com
www.qaranc.co.uk
www.hampshirechronicle.co.uk
www.ghostpubs.com
www.ghostisland.com

Lightning Source UK Ltd.
Milton Keynes UK
UKHW020648270519
343383UK00013B/1806/P